Is Your Organization a Great Workplace?

Is Your Organization a Great Workplace?

Daniel Wentland

≡IAP

INFORMATION AGE PUBLISHING, INC.
Charlotte, NC • www.infoagepub.com

Library of Congress Cataloging-in-Publication Data

The CIP data for this book can be found on the Library of Congress website (loc.gov).

Paperback: 978-1-68123-128-0
Hardcover: 978-1-68123-129-7
E-Book: 978-1-68123-130-3

Printed in the United States of America

CONTENTS

ACKNOWLEDGEMENTS

First, I want to express my appreciation to the readers; I look forward to hearing your comments. Please contact me at daniel@danielwentland.com

Next, a big thanks to George and his crew at Information Age for taking the chance on this book.

Thanks to my editor, Dr. Andrew Kelly.

On a personal note, I appreciate everything my dad did for me.

Finally, my days are always brighter with Kathy, Dakota, Scarlett, and Hailey.

PREFACE

The following tale is from *Zapp! The Lightning of Empowerment* by William Byham and Jeff Cox (1988):

> *Ralph worked in Department N of the Normal Company in Normalburg, USA. For years, Normal had been a leading manufacturer of normalators, those amazing devices which are so fundamental to society as we know it.*
>
> *As you might expect, just about everything was normal at Normal, including the understanding of who was normally supposed to do what:*
>
> *Managers did the thinking*
>
> *Supervisors did the talking*
>
> *And employees did the doing*
>
> *That was the way it had always been—ever since Norman had invented the normalator and founded the company—and so everybody just assumed that was the way it should always be.*
>
> *Ralph was your normal type of employee. He came to work. He did the job his supervisor told him to do. And at the end of the day he dragged himself home to get ready to do it all again.*

When friends or family asked him how he liked his work, Ralph would say, "Oh, it's all right, I guess. Not very exciting, but I guess that's normal. Anyway, it's a job and the pay is OK."

In truth, working for the Normal Company was not very satisfying for Ralph, though he was not sure why. The pay was more than OK; it was good. The benefits were fine, the working conditions were safe. Yet something seemed to be missing.

But Ralph figured there wasn't much he could do to change things at Normal. After all, he reasoned, who would even bother to listen? So at work he kept his thoughts to himself, and just did what he was told. (pp. 3–4)

The Normal Company is typical of many organizations, an okay place to work, but certainly not a great place to work. In organizations like the Normal Company, employees summarize their employment situation by stating, "There are worse places to work."

As a researcher, I spend my time formulating principles designed to enhance the performance of organizations by establishing an effective and efficient workplace. On the other hand, practitioners have the ability to implement principles, policies, practices, theories, and so forth. A critical question for practitioners is: What workflow processes and policies have been implemented in the workplace, and would the stakeholders associated with your organization describe your institution as a great place to work and an effective and efficient organization?

The elements of a great place to work that are outlined in this book will start the process of making your organization a more productive and competitive institution; and make no mistake about it, gaining a competitive advantage in the marketplace can be the difference between organizational sustainability and economic failure.

By the way, great places to work are quite rare, and when you find one you know it, for it's like a beautiful, sparkling diamond. All the employees shine with an enthusiasm that can't be contained, for they understand the unique environment in which they work.

Never forget the truism that "people respond to what is around them" (Crosby, 1986, p. 179); the information in this book will help every reader understand what it truly means to develop a great place to work by examining the elements of a great place to work.

Greatness requires great achievements, and the issue becomes how greatness can be best achieved—the Normal Company approach or the great place to work approach?

INTRODUCTION

Creating a great workplace is generally about crafting an environment built upon striving for excellence, developing collaboration, fostering trust, respecting all, and rewarding merit at the individual, group, and organizational level.

However, underneath everything, we must never forget that a great workplace is first and foremost all about the people who work in the organization. How the managers and non-managerial employees relate to one another impacts the morale of the workforce and the effort that each employee is willing to exert.

Have you ever worked for an organization where it felt like no one cared about you and that your contribution to the organization was always minimized or worse, unappreciated? Unfortunately, I have worked for many organizations where senior officials thought they were the greatest things on earth and everyone else was there to do their bidding. The message emanating throughout that institution consisted of fear and intimidation. Each employee dreaded every work day, and very few employees went beyond what was required to do their jobs. Just trying to make it to Friday was the fuel that kept the workers going. Working for an organization like that can be labeled dispiriting, to say the least.

In contrast, being employed in an organization where each employee understands the important role that he or she plays is a powerful economic factor that separates great organizations from mediocre and plain bad places to work.

In this book, the chapters are designed to move us towards a complete understanding of what a great workplace is, how to develop such an organization, and how to measure whether your organization is a great workplace. The writing is concise and straightforward and leads us on a journey of how to increase the probability of organizational sustainability and how to develop a better awareness of who we are, for not every person wants to create a great workplace.

Many organizational decision makers and practitioners talk about developing a great workplace, but few actually move beyond the talk. It is very common for individuals in positions of power to make statements about how great it is to work in the organization, while the rest of the employees know the "real" work situation.

So let's start our journey of moving beyond words and discover what it takes to turn words into reality and actually transform your organization into a great workplace.

PART 1

THE ELEMENTS OF A GREAT WORKPLACE

Do no harm.
        —*Peter Drucker's advice (Twomey, Jennings, & Fox, 2005, p. 49)*

CHAPTER 1

FUNDAMENTAL CONCEPTS OF A GREAT WORKPLACE?

Broadly, the term *organization* refers to a group of people working together to attain common goals. Researchers have tried to understand the nature of an organization by utilizing a variety of descriptions and analytical approaches, a summary of which is contained in my previous books, *Strategic Training: Putting Employees First* and *Organizational Performance in a Nutshell.* For this book, we can simply state that from the body of research devoted to studying organizational development, three common elements have been cited to describe an organization: (1) people, (2) a goal or purpose, and (3) a structure (meaning any phenomena created by the members of an organization) that defines roles and positions and processes and limits the behavior of members of an organization. Put simply, without people, a goal or purpose, and some form of structure, there is no organization! Of the three elements of an organization, *people* constitute the most important factor, because without human beings, the other two elements cease to exist.

Once the three elements of an organization are brought together and an organization is formed, a culture develops. Two of the most comprehensive definitions of organizational culture are listed below:

3

> The pattern of basic assumptions that a given group has invented, discovered, or developed in learning to cope with its problems of external adaptation and internal integration. (Schein, 1985, p. 14)

> A set of symbols, ceremonies, and myths that communicate the underlying values and beliefs of that organization to its employees. (Ouchi, 1981, p. 41)

Organizational culture is important because organizational culture influences the bottom line. Any individual who has held an administrative position knows that financial results are closely monitored. It does not matter if an organization is described as profit, nonprofit, mechanistic, organic, a matrix structure, or any other description—the bottom line is the bottom line. For our purposes, the definition of "the bottom line" will be a broad one: any financial measurement relating to an organization (e.g., profit or loss, return on total assets, stock price, revenue or market share growth, or return on equity).

So what is the bottom line regarding the impact of organizational culture? Numerous books and studies have demonstrated that the culture of an organization impacts organizational success or failure; therefore, the critical question is: What type of organizational culture or work environment will best support organizational sustainability?

If we define sustainability as the "capacity of a system to engage in the complexities of continuous improvement consistent with deep values of human purpose" (Fullan, 2005, p. ix) and consider a Normal Company approach as described in the preface or a great workplace approach, it becomes obvious which approach can better achieve organizational sustainability as well as organizational greatness. Creating a great workplace can elevate an organization above the competition by creating a more productive workforce and all the economic advantages and benefits that flow from a knowledgeable, highly skilled, and motivated workforce. The issue now becomes how to craft a great workplace.

THE START OF A GREAT WORKPLACE

Developing a great workplace begins with the notion of a norm of reciprocity. Gouldner (1960) suggested that a norm of reciprocity imposes two interrelated demands. The first is that people should help those individuals who helped them, and secondly, people should not injure individuals who have helped them. Similarly, social exchange theory posits that individuals will demonstrate greater commitment to an organization when they feel supported and fairly rewarded. In other words, individuals will form relationships with those who can provide valued resources, and in exchange, those individuals will reciprocate by providing their resources and support (Umback, 2007).

Another concept at the heart of a great workplace is the economic idea of an efficiency wage. An efficiency wage is a wage higher than the wage that equates quantity supplied and quantity demanded or a wage higher than the market clearing wage. Or, as economists would state, an efficiency wage is a wage higher than the equilibrium wage.

Generally, a firm would decide to pay an efficiency wage to lower overall labor costs. How can firms reduce overall labor costs by paying a higher wage? First, fewer workers will be required to produce output; second, workers increase their work effort because they do not want to lose their job because similar alternative employment positions will pay less; third, a firm will experience a lower employee turnover rate and therefore reduce the costs associated with hiring and training employees; and finally, a firm can be more selective in terms of a worker's knowledge, skills, and abilities. A firm that pays an efficiency wage can hire better qualified workers, meaning the employees are more knowledgeable, highly skilled, and more capable of performing the job. The bottom line is the more productive an employee is, the less inefficient the worker is. The final result is higher output at lower overall costs.

As stated by Ari Haseotes, the president and chief operating officer of Cumberland Farms, when turnover is high, customer satisfaction suffers (Weber, 2013). When turnover is high, employee costs increase, employee performance is diminished, customer service is provided at a minimum level at best, and organizational sustainability and greatness is in serious jeopardy.

For clarification purposes, if all organizations offered an efficiency wage, the positive effects of providing an efficiency wage would be negated with the end result being higher unemployment because wages above the equilibrium or market clearing wage always creates unemployment. However, for strategic, economic, and other managerial reasons, not all organizations will pay an efficiency wage; thus, the organizations that do can reap the economic and organizational benefits associated with paying an efficiency wage.

Besides an efficiency wage, merit pay at the individual, group, and organizational level is a critical component of a great workplace. How many of us have worked at an institution where employee performance really did not matter? Whether your work was outstanding and far superior to that of others or whether you did the minimum that was required, or something less than the minimum, all employees basically received the same pay increase. John Kenneth Galbraith once said, "I am puzzled as to why a merit system is important in the absence of merit" (Galbraith & Goodman, 1998, p. 72). Employee performance is a critical element impacting organizational success and employee performance at the individual, group or department, and organizational level must be rewarded according to effort exerted. Keep in mind that merit pay by itself does not reflect a great workplace; however, it is a necessary ingredient of a great workplace.

THE RIGHT ACTION PRINCIPLE

Norm of reciprocity, social exchange theory, efficiency wage, and merit pay at the individual, group or department, and organizational level are encapsulated within the right action principle. A great workplace is built upon the right action principle meaning that pursuing organizational goals and objectives should be conducted in such a manner that growth and the integrity of people are respected (Johnston cited by Seyfarth, 2005).

I will modify the right action principle and state that the concept means never attempting to achieve organizational goals at the expense of the employees. Put simply, organizations that plan every action around their employees increase the probability of thriving in the marketplace as opposed to organizations that view employees as mere costs to be reduced in times of trouble. Making the right action principle the cornerstone of your organizational culture, strategy, structure, processes, and policies is a key test of whether your organization can ever be a great workplace. Unfortunately, most organizations fail the test.

SUMMING IT UP

> The dictionary definition of organization—"a number of persons or groups…united for some purpose of work"—expresses its essential character. The participants, to one degree or another, have submitted to the purposes of organization in pursuit of some common purpose, which then normally involves the winning of the submission of people or groups external to the organization. (Galbraith, 1983, p. 55)

Great places to work increase the probability of winning the submission of people or groups external to the organization. In other words, great places to work are better able to attract and retain loyal customers and are in a more competitive position to achieve the ultimate organizational objective of sustainability in the marketplace.

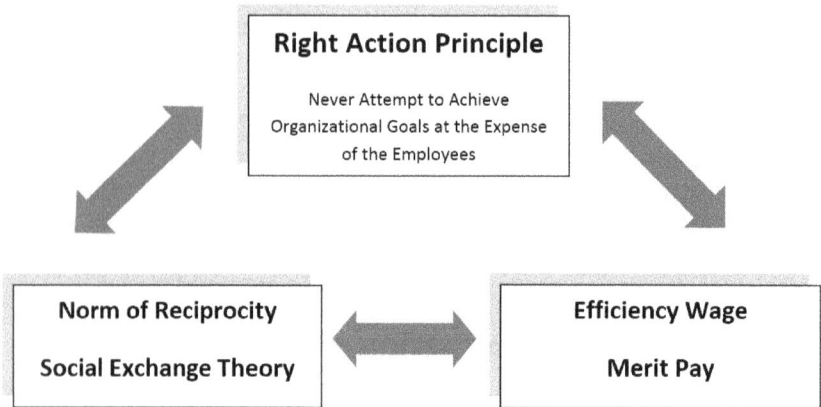

Right Action Principle

Never Attempt to Achieve
Organizational Goals at the Expense
of the Employees

Norm of Reciprocity

Social Exchange Theory

Efficiency Wage

Merit Pay

FIGURE 1.1.   A Great Workplace

CHAPTER 2

DEVELOPING AN ORGANIZATIONAL CULTURE "A" INSTITUTION AND PUTTING EMPLOYEES FIRST

In the first chapter we examined the fundamental concepts of a great workplace. However, to fully comprehend what constitutes a great workplace we must venture forward by introducing the additional elements of such a unique workplace. Our first step in that direction begins with an analysis of an organizational culture "A" institution.

To gain an insight into the dynamics of an organizational culture "A" institution, we must think of an organization as a system consisting of a group of interrelated or interacting elements forming a unified whole that works toward a common goal by accepting inputs and producing outputs in an organized transformation process. A dynamic system essentially has three basic interacting components or functions: an input function that involves capturing and assembling elements that enter the system to be processed, a processing element or transformation process that converts an input into an output, and the output that has been produced. A cybernetic system includes two additional components: feedback and

Is Your Organization a Great Workplace? pages 7–14.
Copyright © 2015 by Information Age Publishing

control. *Feedback* is the data about the performance of a system. *Control* involves monitoring and evaluating feedback to determine whether or not a system is moving toward the achievement of its goal(s). In addition, a system can either be classified as an open system or an adaptive system. An *open system* is a system that interacts with other systems in its environment. An *adaptive system* has the ability to change itself or its environment in order to survive.

Every organization has all three components: input, processing, and output. An effective and efficient organization has all five system components working together as a harmonious whole while having the capacity to interact with other systems and successfully adapt to changes in the marketplace.

If your organization is underperforming, it is the systems that have been established within the organization that are producing those poor results. Unsuccessful organizations are dysfunctional systems. To correct the situation, those systems must be either modified or abandoned (in which case new systems will need to be developed).

ORGANIZATIONS, SYSTEMS, AND CULTURE

Impacting the systems within an organization is the culture of the institution. Organizational culture is a primary factor that explains why one organization succeeds while another entity fails, even though both organizations are producing similar products or services at competitive prices.

To delve deeper into organizational culture, we can use three workplace parameters to help us create a framework for measuring four distinct organizational cultures. These four organizational cultures, in turn, set the stage for the development of the Organizational Culture Financial Status Model (OCFSM). This model can be used to classify and, more importantly, predict the financial status of an organization based on its culture, with the ultimate objective of developing a course of action that will improve the organization's culture and thus its financial situation. The OCFSM is a flexible analytical tool that can be useful in any organizational setting (mechanistic, organic, profit, nonprofit, and so forth). It opens the door to a new perspective of research regarding the quantification of organizational culture by offering a framework for predicting the financial competitiveness of an organization based on the *culture* of the organization, ceteris paribus.

Once we explain the model, we will highlight the connection between organizational culture and the "people factor" within an organization. Ultimately, it's the quality of the people within an organization that will determine the fate of an organization.

SETTING THE STAGE FOR THE OCFSM: WORKPLACE PARAMETERS

The first workplace parameter is managerial attitudes and practices in the workplace. Those attitudes can be assessed by the overall degree of trust or lack of trust between administrative and non-administrative personnel. An adversarial relationship between administrative and non-administrative personnel tends to develop when management focuses too much on operational, financial, and marketing issues while ignoring or paying limited attention to the well-being of employees. Dissatisfied employees purposely engage in many behaviors that limit productivity and compromise organizational success. A fertile breeding ground for advancing productivity and promoting organizational success can only be laid when individuals are respected for who they are and placed in positions that complement their strengths. And make no mistake about it; increasing productivity is the driving force behind economic survival. William J. Baumol and Alan S. Blinder in their 2000 book *Economics: Principles and Policies* put it this way:

> Only rising productivity can raise standards of living in the long run. Over long periods of time, small differences in rates of productivity growth compound like interest in a bank account and can make an enormous difference to a society's prosperity. Nothing contributes more to material well-being, to the reduction of poverty, to increases in leisure time, and to a country's ability to finance education, public health, environmental improvement, and the arts than its productivity growth rate.

From a strict organizational perspective, the right managerial attitude can breathe life into a management philosophy or culture that will boost the chances of organizational success by establishing a workplace environment in which individuals will want to consistently perform at their best.

The second workplace parameter is the organizational environment among the employees. This environment can be assessed by examining the extent of cooperation and internal politics and favoritism within the organization. A highly politicized work environment will eat away at collegiality and undermine productivity. If left unchecked, it will eventually squelch innovation, cripple productivity, and destroy the organization. The long-term survival of any organization will depend on whether or not it controls internal politics and favoritism. Any organization that fails to base performance and compensation on merit will drift into mediocrity and possibly face extinction in the global marketplace. Merit must be rewarded; favoritism must be discouraged.

The third workplace parameter is the tasks being performed within an organization. These tasks can be assessed by asking whether or not they have meaning for the individuals performing them. Individuals tend to be more productive when they sense that their work means something and that they "mean something," and when they feel that their organization is making a positive impact on society. The recent financial scandals at Enron, WorldCom, Qwest, HealthSouth, and others illustrate the negative impact of an organizational culture that fosters unethical behavior. Organizations involved in regulatory or criminal violations or product-liability litigation tend to experience short-term, and in many situations, long-term deterioration in financial performance.

A culture of what Alan Greenspan, former chairman of the Federal Reserve, calls "infectious greed" eventually cripples an organization. On the other hand, organizations that create an environment where individuals feel that their work is important and that their organization is providing a positive benefit to the community set the stage for innovation and creativity. When innovation and creativity flourish, so will productivity—the driving force behind economic growth and survival.

MEASURING ORGANIZATIONAL CULTURE

How do we measure culture? Using the three critical workplace parameters of attitude, environment, and tasks, we can establish criteria for measuring four distinct organizational cultures. Then we can assess the financial status of that organization.

Managerial Attitudes and Practices in the Workplace

Individuals tend to trust the administration when operational, financial, marketing, and employee satisfaction issues are given equal attention by management.

Individuals tend to distrust the administration when management focuses on operational, financial, and marketing issues, yet ignores employee satisfaction issues or gives them only limited attention.

The Organizational Environment

The ideal environment is one in which cooperation among individuals and departments/units is encouraged, politicking and favoritism are discouraged, and performance and compensation issues are based on merit.

An atmosphere of noncooperation exists when cooperation among individuals and departments/units is discouraged, politicking and favoritism are encouraged, and performance and compensation issues are not based on merit.

The Tasks Being Performed Within an Organization

The task has meaning to the individual when he or she feels that his or her actions have a meaningful impact on the organization. The individual should feel that the organization stands for something more than just the pursuit of profits— that it also contributes to the welfare of the community. In addition, the organization must pursue ethical behavior in accomplishing its daily and long-term strategic objectives.

Tasks do not have meaning if individuals feel that their actions have no meaningful impact on the organization, the organization does not stand for something more than just the pursuit of profits, and the organization encourages a culture of infectious greed.

With our measurement criteria established, we can now see four distinct organizational cultures and institutions:

An Organizational Culture "A" Institution:
- There is a relationship of trust between administrative and non-administrative personnel.
- Cooperation between individuals and departments/units is encouraged, and politicking and favoritism are discouraged.
- Individuals feel that their actions have a meaningful impact on the organization.

An Organizational Culture "C" Institution:
- Two of the three elements of organizational culture "A" are present (e.g., trust and cooperation). However, the tasks might not have meaning for the individual.

An Organizational Culture "D" Institution:
- One of the three elements of organizational culture "A" is present (e.g., the tasks might have meaning for the individual, but there is no trust or cooperation present within the culture of the organization).

An Organizational Culture "F" Institution:
- None of the three elements of organizational culture "A" are present.

Now that we have identified four measurable and distinct organizational cultures and institutions, we can present the OCFSM (Figure 2.1).

According to the OCFSM, organizations that have a type "A" culture are predicted to outperform their competition. Financial measurements that can be used to test this assumption include earnings per share, sales volume, return on equity, stock price, operational costs, and net profit. As for policy recommendations, the OCFSM suggests that administrative personnel should continue with their current practices.

Organizations that have a type "C" culture are predicted to be financially competitive with other organizations within the same industry. The policy recommendation for these organizations is to incorporate within their organizational culture the missing organizational culture "A" element, and thus form a type "A" culture.

Organizations that have a type "D" culture are predicted to perform below their competitors. The policy recommendation for these organizations is to develop a type "C" or "A" organizational culture.

Organizations that have a type "F" culture are predicted to perform significantly below their competitors. The policy recommendation for these organizations is to incorporate the missing elements of organizational cultures "C" or "A."

An Organizational Culture "A" Institution
Measurement Criteria (Trust exists, Cooperation is present, Task has meaning)
Financial Status of the Organization (Higher financial performance compared to other organizations within the same industry)
Recommended Course of Action (Continue present policies and practices)

An Organizational Culture "C" Institution
Measurement Criteria (Two of the three elements of organizational culture "A" are present)
Financial Status of the Organization (Competitive financial performance compared to other organizations within the same industry- Industry standard position)
Recommended Course of Action (Incorporate the missing element of organizational culture "A" into the "C" culture)

An Organizational Culture "D" Institution
Measurement Criteria (One of the three elements of organizational culture "A" is present)
Financial Status of the Organization (Below average financial performance compared to other organizations within the same industry)
Recommended Course of Action (Incorporate the two missing elements of organizational culture "A" into the "D" culture)

An Organizational Culture "F" Institution
Measurement Criteria (Distrust, Non-cooperation, Task does not have meaning)
Financial Status of the Organization (Significantly below-average financial performance, compared to other organizations within the same industry)
Recommended Course of Action (Incorporate the three missing elements of organizational culture "A" into the "F" culture

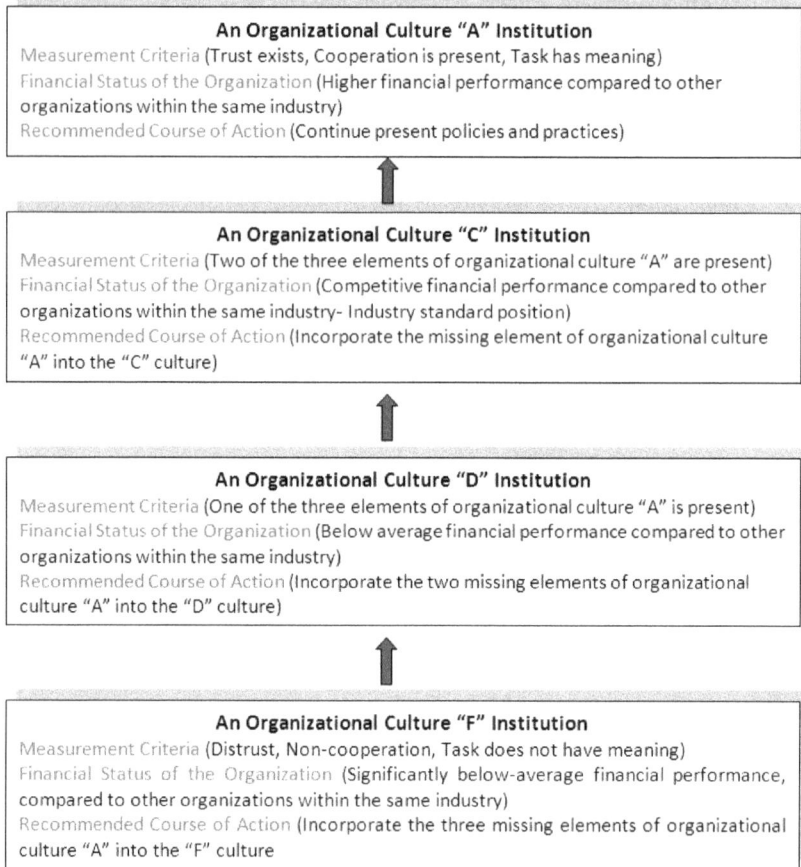

FIGURE 2.1. Organizational Culture Financial Status Model (OCFSM)

THE OCFSM AND THE BOTTOM LINE

The financial status model, OCFSM, links the culture of an organization and the financial status of that organization. In addition, the model provides decision makers with a methodology to improve the financial status of their organization by adopting an administrative philosophy that fosters a type "A" organizational culture or at least an organizational culture "C" workplace. It elevates the analysis regarding organizational culture by quantifying the culture of an organization in order to predict its financial performance, while also providing a course of action to improve the organization's culture and thus its bottom line. In the final analysis, this is what business is all about!

THE OCFSM AND THE "PEOPLE FACTOR,

Organizational cultures A, C, D, and F provide a framework for understanding organizational performance—a framework built on three critical workplace parameters: managerial attitudes and practices in the workplace, the organizational environment among the employees, and the tasks being performed within an organization.

At the core of the OCFSM lies a common thread that binds each of the three critical workplace parameters together. This common thread is the driving force that ultimately determines whether or not an organization will possess an A, C, D, or F organizational culture, so it has a fundamental influence on the level of success an organization can achieve. So what is this common thread? The "people" element is the most important factor in any organization. The quality and attitudes of the people within an organization set the stage for its accomplishments. Thus, to understand organizational performance, one must understand the "people factor" within an organization.

In sum, the quality of an organization's people, at all levels, determines organizational success or failure because an organization is nothing more than the system(s) that the members of the organization created, and the superiority of any creation ultimately depends on the abilities of its creator(s). Thus, at the core of organizational performance is the quality of the members of an organization. Failing to recognize this truism leaves the organization in peril.

PUTTING EMPLOYEES FIRST

In association with the OCFSM and an organizational culture "A" institution is my employment principle of putting employees first.

In a *Wall Street Journal* article, it was reported that most organizations do not practice what they preach, despite the claims of a majority of executives that their organizations treat employees with respect and offer fair pay for the tasks performed (Kent, 2005). The disconnection between what organizations say they believe and what they actually do is partly attributable to a marketing philosophy that began to dominate management theory after the production concept faded in popularity in the 1950s to 1960s. At the center of this philosophy is the notion that *the customer* should be the focus of all organizational activities and planning.

Although the emphasis upon the customer appears to be a logical premise for building organizational success, it is actually quite misleading: Simply put, many organizations do not know who their customers are! For example, who is the customer at a college or university? High school graduates? Adults returning to college? Graduate students? Individuals from other countries attending classes? Or individuals seeking a vocational trade? And what are the socioeconomic and demographic data associated with these classifications of students? Who is the customer for a retailer like Wal-Mart? Is it the person who drives a Mercedes to Wal-Mart in order to purchase everyday items at lower prices? Or is it the individual who uses public transportation to arrive at the store? A customer who cannot be specifically identified in every detail is an illusion, and illusions serve as a poor basis for building successful strategy.

And once the "customer" has been identified, should he or she be placed at the center of every organizational activity? Doing so, I believe, pushes aside the true essence of the organization, minimizing its significance. The heart of an organization is its employees (managerial and non-managerial). The abilities, decisions, plans, training, and actions of the employees of an organization are what draw individuals to a particular college or retailer or even to purchase a product or pay for a service. The primary driving force that brings people into a concert hall is to hear enchanting music performed by trained musicians whose skills and talents are on display. Highly qualified employees produce quality products and provide quality service that satisfies consumer needs.

An organization's employees have always made the difference between a truly successful organization and a mediocre entity, but it's amazing how often managers overlook or discount this fundamental recipe for economic survival. My premise here is that an organization that plans every action around its employees will thrive in the marketplace. The Wegman's chain of grocery stores headquartered in Rochester, New York, has repeatedly been cited as one of the best employers in the United States to work for. The company's focus on its employees has made Wegman's a shining example of a local, family-managed organization that effectively and efficiently competes against national and international grocery chains.

SUMMING IT UP

Developing an Organizational Culture "A" institution and putting employees first are underlying foundations of a great workplace. As stated by Randy Best, "We believe that success in any venture, for profit or not profit, depends on the quality of people" (Manzo, 2006, p. 20).

CHAPTER 3

THE RIGHT LEADERSHIP

Let's pause to recap before moving on. At this point in our journey, we have come to realize that a great workplace has its roots firmly embedded within the human relations notion of a norm of reciprocity, social exchange theory, and the economic principles of an efficiency wage and merit pay. However, just as all the matter in the universe originated from the big bang, the primordial beginning of a great workplace is the right action principle. Additionally, a great workplace must foster a type "A" organizational culture and embrace the managerial philosophy of putting employees first (see Figure 3.1).

The bottom line from everything that has been exposed so far is that a great workplace requires a different perspective about what is important in order to achieve organizational greatness and sustainability. To be frank, talking about being a great workplace and really creating one are two very different circumstances. Talk is cheap; actions are what count.

In the management literature there is the notion of "X" and "Y" employees. Generally, X-type employees are viewed as lazy and management needs to constantly watch over the employees to make sure that something gets done while Y-type employees are eager to work and require minimum supervision. The same idea can be applied to management: There are "X" and "Y" managers and leaders. X-type managers are controlling and self-absorbed among other negative managerial tendencies, while Y-type managers and leaders are the opposite. As we will

Is Your Organization a Great Workplace? pages 15–21.

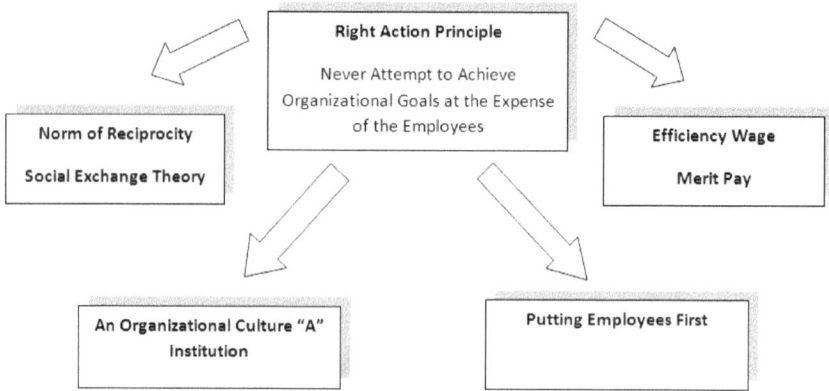

FIGURE 3.1.   A Great Workplace

soon see, in a workplace supervised by X-type managers, the life blood of a great workplace is drained away, just like a vampire sucking the life out of a victim. A great workplace will never exist under the same roof where X-type managers and leaders exist.

GAINING A BETTER UNDERSTANDING OF X-TYPE AND Y-TYPE MANAGERS AND LEADERS

Let's consider two individuals. The first person is (1) highly materialistic; (2) always focused upon his needs; (3) not concerned about how goals are achieved as long as they are accomplished; (4) only concerned with the here and now; (5) insensitive towards the physical environment, meaning at the macro level, the Earth, and at the micro level, the workplace; (6) not interested in anyone else's point of view; (7) power driven; and finally (8) constantly favoring certain individuals. The second person has the opposite characteristics.

Which individual would you prefer as a boss? I don't believe anyone of us would select the first individual, and if you were unfortunate enough to have to work for a person like that, how much effort do you put forth? The first individual has the characteristics associated with an egocentric view of life. The second person has adopted an altruistic view of life. The right type of leader must possess an altruistic perspective of life, for only that kind of person will have the characteristics that are necessary to inspire others to want to do their best (see Figure 3.2).

An egocentric person is primarily consumed with satisfying his or her own needs. An altruistic person focuses upon the interests of others and as a result gains the trust and loyalty of those who work for him or her. It is that bond of trust and loyalty between the altruistic leader and the employees that sets the foundation for obtaining extraordinary organizational results. Put simply, in terms

Perception Personality Attitudes Motivation	→	Two Approaches To Life Egocentric <u>and</u> Altruistic	→	The right type of leader walks upon the altruistic path of life and has the values and character that can stimulate others to accomplish organizational goals that are far beyond the reach of anyone who follows the egocentric path of life.

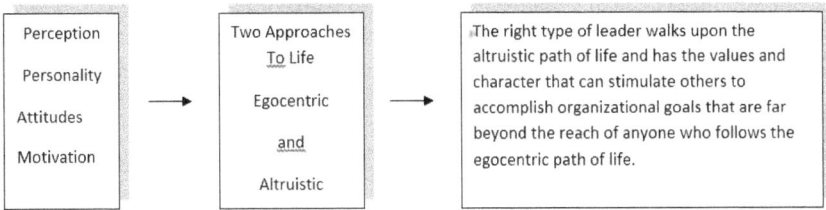

FIGURE 3.2.   Understanding Who We Are and in the Process Discovering the Right Type of Leader

of achieving organizational greatness and sustainability, an individual with an egocentric approach to life will in the long run never measure up to a person with an altruistic viewpoint.

But what exactly is leadership? Unfortunately a straightforward definition has proven elusive, for leadership has been defined in many ways by many individuals:

- Leadership is both a process and a property. As a process, leadership involves the use of non-coercive influences. As a property, leadership is the set of characteristics attributed to someone who is perceived to use influence successfully. (Moorhead & Griffin, 1995)
- Leadership is the process whereby one person influences others to work toward a goal and helps them pursue a vision. (Yulk & VanFleet, cited by Hellriegel, Slocum, & Woodman, 1995)
- Leadership is the process of guiding and motivating others toward the achievement of organizational goals. (Gitman & McDaniel, 2003)
- Strategic leadership refers to the ability to articulate a strategic vision for the company, or a part of the company, and to motivate others to buy into that vision. (Hill & Jones, 1998)
- Leadership is the ability to influence a group toward the achievement of goals. (Robbins, 2001)
- Leadership…is the ability to get other people to get the very best out of themselves. And it is manifested…not by getting them to follow you, but by getting them to join you. You don't get the best out of people by bulldozing them; you do it by educating (or convincing) them. (Levy, 2004)

And the list can go on and on, but in the end, the definition isn't important. What matters is that you are the right type of leader, a Y-type manager or leader and an individual who is guided by the right action principle. The specific characteristics of the right type of leader include the following:

- The right type of leader has the right self-image and self-concept to want to create a workplace in which the traditional management–employee relationship paradigm is cast aside in favor of the new management–employee paradigm where employees are regarded as partners, not subordinates; in other words, management must put employees first—and mean it. Management retains the final decision-making authority, but the focus should be upon how an organizational decision impacts the employees, for that in turn will influence how the employees perform their jobs and ultimately how they interact with the customer.
- The right type of leader can easily adapt to various situations and is sociable, conscientious, tactful, considerate, and open to various points of view.
- The right type of leader is not focused upon what he or she can gain but instead is concerned about the conditions of all those individuals who work for him or her. By truly caring about the employees, the right type of leader will achieve unparalleled organizational success. In other words, the right type of leader makes a true commitment to the employees and it's that commitment that inspires the employees to want to accomplish organizational goals in the most effective and efficient manner (social exchange theory).
- The right type of leader embraces change, whether it is small or large, whenever it is necessary to do so. In fact the right type of leader actively promotes an organizational culture that has an enhanced capacity to learn, adapt, and change.
- The right type of leader must possess an altruistic perspective of life, for only that kind of person has the characteristics to inspire others to want to do their best.
- The right type of leader pursues organizational goals and objectives in such a way that the growth and integrity of people are respected.

Now let's compare the characteristics of the right type of leader with a leadership style that flows from an egocentric perspective of life and can best be described as a CREEP approach to leadership or the X-type of manager or leader.

- CREEPS are *control freaks*. A CREEP makes all the decisions and only makes a token or superficial effort to seek employee input or suggestions. CREEPS are the ultimate micromanagers. Anything not initiated by the CREEP is rejected.
- CREEPS *form relationships with favorite employees*; work performance is secondary. Only those in the inner circle of the CREEP are allowed any involvement in the day-to-day managerial activities of the organization.
- CREEPS *have king- or queen-size egos* and view employees as cogs in a machine that can be easily replaced. CREEPS have none or very little concern for employees except for the CREEP's favorite employees. CREEPS utilize HR policies to intimidate and severely limit employee empowerment.

- CREEPS *have limited ethics*. CREEPS utilize a Machiavellian approach to getting tasks accomplished. CREEPS are abusive and manipulative. CREEPS are only concerned about themselves and view others as human pawns that can be used as the CREEP sees fit; any employee development will only occur if it benefits the CREEP.
- CREEPS *love power* and institute a top-down managerial philosophy. CREEPS are not interested in developing future leaders because those individuals are viewed by CREEPS as threats. CREEPS love to show off their power.
- CREEPS *are as secretive as possible*. CREEPS don't like to share information with employees. Employees find out information through the grapevine. When a CREEP does have to share information with employees, it's communicated through formal communication channels, and generally the employees are not allowed (or only superficially allowed) to be part of the decision-making process.

The difference between the right type of leader (Y-type manager or leader) and a CREEP (X-type manager or leader) can also be illustrated by slightly modifying the work of Peters and Austin (1985).

A Description of the Right Type of Leader (Y-type Manager or Leader) Includes:

- Comfortable with people
- Puts employees first
- Open-door cheerleader
- No reserved parking place, private washroom, or dining room
- Common touch
- Good listener
- Fair
- Humble
- Tough, confronts nasty problems
- Tolerant of disagreement (respectful of the opinion of others)
- Has strong convictions (altruistic approach to life)
- Trusts people
- Gives credit, takes blame
- Prefers personal communication over written communication such as memos, email, or long reports
- Keeps promises
- Thinks there are at least two other people in the organization who would be good CEOs

The Description of a CREEP (X-type Manager or Leader) Is as Follows:

- Uncomfortable with people
- Puts his or her needs first, not the needs of the employees
- Generally inaccessible to employees
- Has a reserved parking place, private washroom, and dining area
- Strained relationship with employees
- Good talker in terms of outlining what they want, poor listener
- Fair to favorite employees, exploit the rest
- Arrogant
- Avoid nasty problems, elusive, the artful dodger
- Intolerant of disagreement, does not respect the opinion of others
- No firm stand, vacillates and utilizes a Machiavellian approach
- Distrusts employees and focuses upon numbers on reports
- Takes credit, blames others for failures
- Prefers written communication over personal contact
- Does not keep promises
- Makes sure that no one is hired who remotely resembles a CEO (or a challenge to their authority)

In terms of organizational performance, which leadership style will achieve maximum performance? I think it's quite obvious that an organization with the right type of leaders will outperform an organization filled with CREEPS because the right type of leaders can tap the full potential of the workforce.

SUMMING IT UP

When it's all said and done, how can we capture the essence of being the right type of leader? The right leadership is always focused upon the right action principle; strives for excellence; keeps procedures, policies, and structure as straightforward as possible—in other words, follows the KISS principle of Keep It Simple Stupid, creates a collaborative workplace—not top-down, and develops the full potential of an organization's most important asset—the employees (managerial and non-managerial).

In the final analysis, leadership and organizational greatness and sustainability are forever locked in an eternal struggle against the numerous forces in today's highly competitive marketplace, an economic battle that can destroy an organization at any moment. The critical role of leadership can best be summarized by the following story that was told by Dr. Ronald Walker during a doctoral class that I was taking at Jackson State University:

You can learn a lot about leadership by watching a farmer trying to get a group of cows to move from one pasture to another. The farmer can get behind the cows and try to push them in the direction he wants the cows to go. Eventually the farmer will

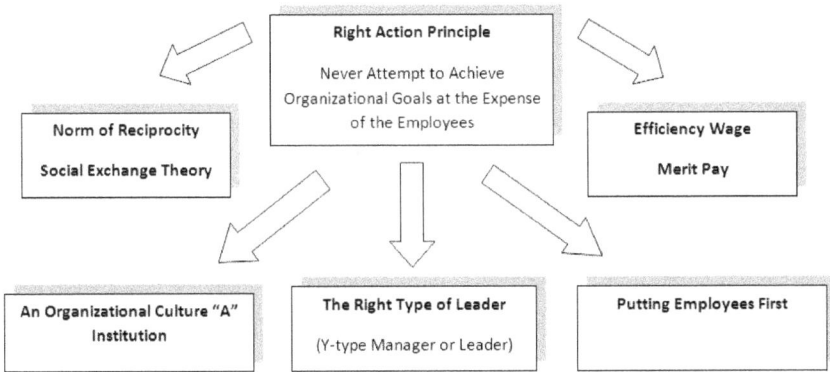

FIGURE 3.3. A Great Workplace

get the cows into the next pasture; however, he would have spent a lot of time and used a lot of effort in the process. Instead of trying to push the cows, the farmer could have observed which cow was the lead cow and placed a bucket of feed in front of that cow and easily, with minimum effort, led that cow, and subsequently the other cows, out of one gate and through another into a new pasture. However, what we must always be careful of is who has the bucket and where he is leading us. It could be to the slaughterhouse.

With the right type of leader (a Y-type manager or leader) no one needs to worry about the direction in which the organization is heading, for that decision would have been mutually agreed upon between management and the employees. Ultimately it's the values and character of the right type of leader that are grounded within an altruistic approach to life that will allow for the creation of a productive workplace characterized by motivated employees who are always willing to do their best for the customer. That's the kind of organization that will survive the rigors of the marketplace and achieve greatness and sustainability.

CHAPTER 4

EFFECTIVE MANAGEMENT

Why does one organization appeal to consumers while others struggle to attract customers even though both are operating in the same industry? How can organizational performance be outstanding one year and average or worse the following year? Why does a company with a quality product fail in the marketplace? Why are so many individuals disappointed with their work environment? What drives productivity and value creation? What distinguishes a great workplace from an ordinary or miserable one? What determines organizational performance? How can some of the largest global organizations such as Bank of America, Sears, Kmart, Borders, Citigroup, J.C. Penney, Kodak, and Dell perform so poorly after being such colossal leaders in their industry?

All these questions represent a small sample of the critical topics that management and leadership experts grapple with in their quest to understand the forces that impact organizational performance. In 1961, Harold Koontz summarized the various research approaches that have evolved to address organizational, managerial, and leadership issues. Koontz divided these investigative approaches into six schools of thought.

- The first category of scholarship is known as the management process school. Fathered by Henri Fayol, this school of thought examines the functions of management (planning, organizing and staffing, leading, and controlling) in an attempt to improve the management process.

- The empirical school of thought analyzes real-world cases in the hope of determining what works and what does not in certain situations. Ernest Dale's comparative approach would be an example of this line of inquiry.
- The human behavior school studies how the behavior of individuals impacts organizational outcomes. The premise of this school is that the study of management should focus upon interpersonal relationships since managing involves working with people in order to accomplish certain tasks and organizational goals.
- The social system school utilizes system theory to understand group and organizational performance. Major contributors to this school include Chester Barnard and Herbert Simon.
- The decision theory school can be characterized by its concentration on the decision-making process and the belief that the development of management theory should primarily focus upon analyzing and improving that process.
- The mathematical school views management as a field of study that can be evaluated and improved through the use of mathematical models.

The problem with viewing organizational performance through a particular school of thought is that the analysis becomes too compartmental, or as stated by Gareth Morgan (1997), "a way of seeing is a way of not seeing." With such a narrow research perspective, what has been lacking is the development of a "macro" or comprehensive approach that combines various elements from each school of thought. It's sort of like trying to piece together a jigsaw puzzle without seeing the entire picture of the puzzle on the front of the box. Without the benefit of seeing the whole picture, the task of fitting together the pieces of the puzzle becomes more difficult. By analyzing organizational performance through a comprehensive framework, a complete picture can emerge that more fully addresses the many unresolved questions relating to organizational success or failure.

From a macro or comprehensive perspective, three primary factors impact organizational survival: (1) the internal environment of an organization, (2) the external environment, and (3) the element of chance that can tilt an organization towards success or failure (see Figure 4.1).

Organizational survival depends upon activities that create an internal environment geared towards achieving a high level of productivity while continually scanning the external environment for conditions that may be favorable to the organization in an attempt to reduce the probability that survival will solely hinge upon the element of chance.

In his ground-breaking book *Future Shock*, Alvin Toffler (1971) described three conditions under which a product can become obsolete. Obsolescence due to function failure occurs when a product physically deteriorates to a point where

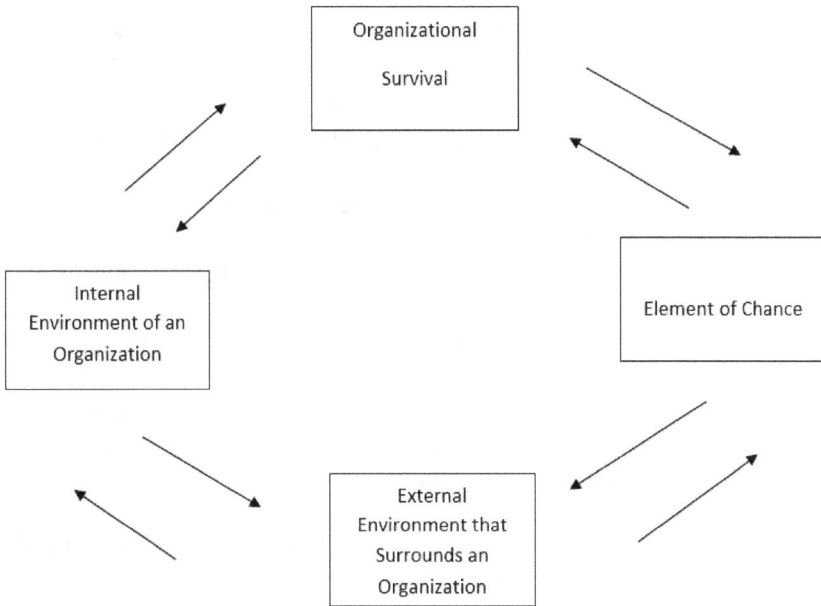

FIGURE 4.1.

the product can no longer be utilized. Substantive technological advance refers to a situation where a new, highly competitive product is offered in the marketplace, causing another similar product to become obsolete. The third condition that causes a product to become obsolete is when it no longer meets the needs of consumers. Similarly, an organization can fall prey to obsolescence, wither, and eventually become extinct, destined to become a faded memory in a business game version of Trivial Pursuit.

When evaluating organizational survival we cannot ignore the truism that how managers choose to utilize their authority in the workplace can have tremendous negative implications upon employee performance and customer satisfaction. For example, according to W. Edwards Deming, long considered the "father of quality control," 85% of all problems in industry could be attributed to "common source of variation," or factors under the control of management and that only 15% resulted from "special causes of variation" or quality problems due to employee/worker errors. Deming insisted that it is up to management to correct system problems and create a workplace environment that promotes quality and enables workers to achieve their full potential. It's the employees who breathe life into an organization, for it's their skills and abilities that give an organization its competitiveness.

My premise is not to blame management for every organizational failure but to suggest that the time has arrived for a paradigm shift in the relationship between management and the employees. Management must come to the realization that organizational performance is enhanced when they view employees as partners, not subordinates; in other words, management must put the employees first—and mean it. The managerial philosophy of putting the employees first and reinforcing that philosophy through the policies and practices established by management is one of the features that distinguish a great workplace from the rest. Management retains the final decision-making authority, but the focus should be upon how an organizational decision impacts the employees, for that in turn will influence how the employees feel about the organization, perform their job, and ultimately how they interact with the customer.

As for the employees, they must continually attempt to increase productivity and strive for excellence in every task they perform as management loosens the grip of power and accepts the employees as equal partners. Put simply, productivity and economic success are achieved through the people of an organization. Changing the management–employee paradigm is an important ingredient in developing a great workplace (Figure 4.2).

How does your organization treat you? Does your organization act as if you are its most important asset or just another cost? How does the culture of your organization impact your work performance?

After studying management, leadership, organizational behavior, marketing, and economics since the 1980s and working in numerous administrative positions, I have come to the conclusion that organizations that establish policies and practices that clearly demonstrate a true concern for the employees have set the

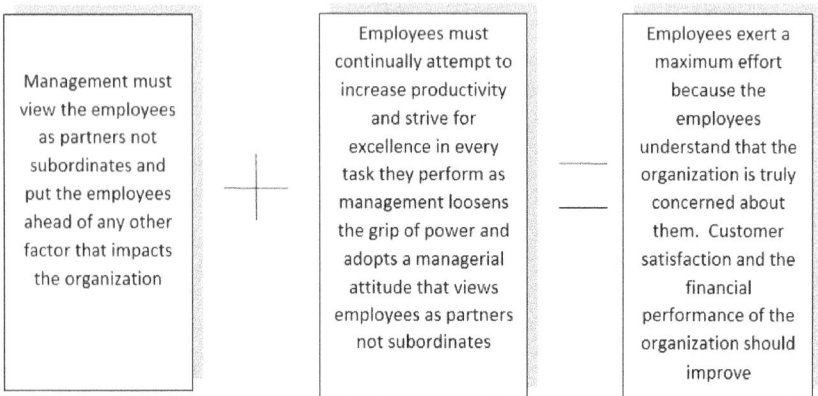

Management must view the employees as partners not subordinates and put the employees ahead of any other factor that impacts the organization	Employees must continually attempt to increase productivity and strive for excellence in every task they perform as management loosens the grip of power and adopts a managerial attitude that views employees as partners not subordinates	Employees exert a maximum effort because the employees understand that the organization is truly concerned about them. Customer satisfaction and the financial performance of the organization should improve

FIGURE 4.2. Changing the Management–Employee Relationship Paradigm

stage where the employees will be more likely to put forth the maximum effort to take care of the customer, not the minimum.

Since organizational survival or death primarily hinges upon the employees (managerial and non-managerial), what management principles can be utilized to foster an effective and efficient workplace?

Effective Management Principles

- In most situations, a participative management style increases the probability of organizational success. Employees should be viewed as partners, not subordinates.
- The best technique to increase motivation is to create a great workplace.
- Motivational gimmicks have little to no impact. In fact, motivational gimmicks might have negative consequences upon morale, motivation, and organizational commitment.
- Individuals will only change their behavior if they want to, and thus it's extremely important to immediately address any personnel issues that have a negative impact on the organization.
- The culture of an organization (and any subculture) should be driven by a managerial philosophy of "putting the employees first" and empowering the employees as much as possible. Organizations that put their employees first will increase the probability of having employees dedicated to providing the best quality products and services for the customer because the employees understand that the organization is willing to put its own survival on the line when it comes to taking care of the employees.
- Putting employees first involves paying an efficiency wage; rewarding individual, group, and organizational level work performance based upon merit; and providing a comprehensive benefits package.
- Putting employees first does not mean that nonperforming employees are not documented and eventually terminated from the organization, if necessary. If a nonperforming employee does not improve his or her performance, then he or she must be dismissed. Nonperforming employees are like a cancer that slowly but surely eats away at organizational performance and success.
- An effective manager, like the right type of leader, is guided by the right action principle.

Bringing about a paradigm shift in the management–employee relationship will not be easy, for many organizations claim to put their employees first, but few do; exceptions include Wegmans and Chick-fil-A. Wegmans, a regional grocery chain headquartered in Rochester, New York, and Chick-fil-A are examples of organizations that are consistently rated as great places to work.

One day while enjoying a delicious Chick-fil-A sandwich, I happened to look at a sign posted on one of the walls of the restaurant. The sign was titled "Never on Sundays," and the words written on the sign describe what it means to be a great workplace:

> People always ask us, "Why are you closed on Sunday?" We respect the hard work of our employees. As a result, we believe in giving them the day off to worship, if they choose, or spend time with family and friends.

Chick-fil-A is a company that moves beyond talking about putting their employees first and actually establishes policies and practices that clearly demonstrate the company's concern for its employees. In terms of improving morale, motivation, productivity, and organizational commitment, it is the actions of management that are what's important, not their words.

SUMMING IT UP

Becoming a great workplace requires having an effective management team. Efficient managers are guided by the following principles:

- Craft an organizational vision and mission that is shared and supported by all stakeholders.
- Build the culture of the organization around the right action principle and putting employees first.
- Create a safe, efficient, and effective workplace.
- Develop a collaborative relationship with local, state, national, and international stakeholders.
- Promote ethical conduct.
- Foster an awareness of the larger cultural, legal, economic, political, and social forces that impact the organization.

FIGURE 4.3. A Great Workplace

CHAPTER 5

COMPLETING THE LEADERSHIP AND MANAGEMENT PICTURE

Flowing from our perceptions and personality are the attitudes or opinions we have adopted. Stephen Laws, a horror novelist, once wrote "A man is what his thoughts are every day" (p. 86). Each of us expresses our thoughts or opinions about everything ranging from a particular coaching decision during a football game to what we think about another person to the quality or worth of a work of art, whether it's a painting, play, sculpture, or musical. Our opinions or attitudes may or may not be based upon any facts, but every attitude has three components. The cognitive component is the intellectual or belief segment of an attitude. The affective component is the feeling or emotional segment of an attitude. The behavioral component is an intention to behave in a certain manner towards someone or something.

Important workplace attitudes include job satisfaction, job involvement, and organizational commitment. An individual with a high level of job satisfaction and job involvement has a positive attitude towards the job and strongly identifies with and cares about the kind of work he does. Individuals with a high level of job satisfaction and job involvement tend to also have a high regard for the organization in terms of loyalty, identification, and organizational involvement.

Is Your Organization a Great Workplace? pages 29–31.
29

A high level of job satisfaction, job involvement, and organizational commitment stems from creating a great workplace and matching the physical and intellectual abilities of an employee with the job. When trying to match the abilities of an employee to the job, it's critical that we understand the characteristics of the job, and a useful tool for accomplishing that is the job characteristics model (JCM). According to the JCM, every job has five core dimensions: skill variety, task identity, task significance, autonomy, and feedback. Skill variety is the degree to which the job requires a variety of different activities. Task identity is the degree to which the job requires completion of a whole and identifiable piece of work. Task significance is the degree to which the job has a substantial impact on the lives or work of other people. Autonomy is the degree to which the job provides substantial freedom and discretion to the individual in scheduling the work and in determining the procedures to be used in carrying it out. Feedback is the degree to which carrying out the work activities results in the individual obtaining feedback about the effectiveness of his or her performance.

When employees are well suited for the job, remarkable levels of productivity can be achieved. Productive employees are motivated employees. Motivation refers to an individual's willingness to exert high levels of effort. Employees are willing and able to exert a high level of effort when the employee ability–job match is in equilibrium, when recognition is provided for accomplishments, and when opportunities for advancement are available for those employees who desire them. A motivated workforce sets the stage for organizational success and sustainability. In today's extremely competitive and global business environment, no organization can expect to achieve sustainability without a highly motivated workforce.

Making a "true" commitment to the employees is the signature of a great workplace and the calling card of the right type of leader, and it's the leader's commitment that inspires the employees to want to accomplish organizational goals in the most efficient and effective manner. In other words, the right type of leader can motivate and lead others towards achieving extraordinary organizational results in the short run and, more importantly, in the long run.

By the way, leadership and management are not the same managerial concepts. I like to think of leadership as doing the right thing while management entails doing the right thing, the right way. Leadership is about providing organizational direction and stimulating high performance among the employees. Management focuses upon the short-term and long-term activities of planning, organizing and staffing, and controlling the production or sales process.

- Planning is evaluating a situation utilizing the strategic planning process, which entails reviewing the strengths and weaknesses of an organization and analyzing the external opportunities and threats (SWOT analysis). The strategic planning process should result in determining the organizational goals that will be pursued and deciding the actions that will be taken to achieve the goals. In its purest form, strategic planning is all about (1) discovering critical factors in a situation and (2) designing a way of coordinating and focusing actions to deal with those critical factors.

- Organizing and staffing includes assembling the human, physical, financial, and informational resources that are necessary to accomplish organizational tasks in an efficient and effective manner.
- Controlling the workplace involves monitoring organizational workflow and taking corrective action if necessary.

A good manager is good at these functions; however, that does not mean that a good manager is a good leader or that a good leader is a good manager. I am sure that all of us have known an individual who was a good manager, but not a good leader and vice-versa. A great workplace has great leaders (the right type of leader, a Y-type leader) and effective managers.

SUMMING IT UP

How can we encapsulate the managerial concepts of leadership, management, and motivation so we do not become lost in all the details?

Both the right type of leader and an effective manager must be guided by the right action principle; however, a leader's job is to help change context, meaning introducing new elements into the situation that influence behavior for the better (Fullan, 2003, p. 1). The right type of leader fosters an organizational culture that (1) strives for excellence; (2) keeps the organizational bureaucracy to a minimum; (3) creates a collaborative workplace, not top-down; and (4) most importantly of all, develops the full potential of each employee (managerial and non-managerial).

An effective manager (1) provides opportunities to achieve high performance; (2) rewards high performance at the individual, group, and organizational level; (3) creates procedures, policies, and structure that establish a positive work environment; (4) removes, in an ethical manner, internal and external barriers that interfere with organizational accomplishments; and (5) develops control systems to monitor organizational progress.

Motivation is about establishing an environment where individuals have the opportunity to grow better every day. Educational reformer Michael Fullan wrote, "There is nothing better that motivates people to make the investment of time, energy, and commitment than to grow better at something that has importance. Failure may be the initial motivator, but it is increased competence that leads us to do more and more" (2007, p. 56).

In the final analysis, a high level of job satisfaction, job involvement, and organizational commitment are a product of combining the right type of leadership with effective management principles.

PART 2

DESCRIPTION AND MEASURING
A GREAT WORKPLACE

CHAPTER 6

WHAT'S A GREAT WORKPLACE LOOK LIKE?

Taking care of first things first—to gain a better understanding of why an organization exists and how it can continue to survive against competing entities—we must venture deep into the realm of strategic planning, decision-making, and value creation.

The role of strategic planning is to keep an organization on track and focused on the activities that it does best so that it does not drift into mediocrity. Strategic planning should improve management decision making and give the company a competitive advantage or allow it to remain competitive in the marketplace. The hallmarks of strategic planning are analysis, development of a course of action aimed at achieving a competitive advantage, implementation of that course of action, constant feedback, and taking corrective measures when necessary. The holy grail of the strategic planning process is to learn how to make better managerial decisions, as measured by the competitive advantage that the organization achieves over its rivals (see Figure 6.1).

Is Your Organization a Great Workplace? pages 35–47.
Copyright © 2015 by Information Age Publishing

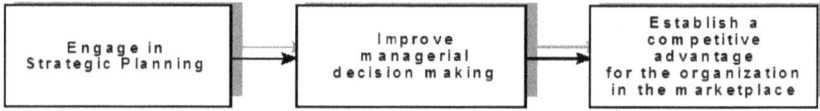

FIGURE 6.1.

MANAGERIAL DECISION MAKING

Systems engineering pioneer Andrew Sage defines managerial decision making as *the processes of thought and action involving an irrevocable allocation of resources that culminates in choice behavior.* "The quality of a decision depends on how well the decision maker is able to acquire information, to analyze information, and to evaluate and interpret information such as to discriminate between relevant and irrelevant bits of data," Sage wrote in 1981. Henry Mintzberg identified four basic roles that managerial decision makers tend to assume in an organization: the *entrepreneur,* who voluntarily initiates change; the *disturbance handler,* who assists in settling disputes; the *resource allocator,* who decides how scarce organizational resources will be distributed; and finally a *negotiator,* who represents the organization in reaching agreements with other organizations. The quality of the decision is influenced by skills that the manager possesses. Most successful managers have a battery of technical, interpersonal, conceptual, and diagnostic skills that they use quite effectively (Figure 6.2).

- Technical skills: Skills necessary to accomplish specific tasks within the organization

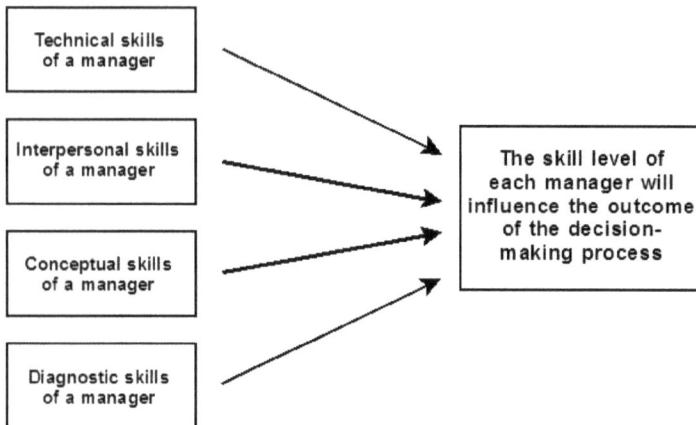

FIGURE 6.2.

- Interpersonal skills: Skills that make up the manager's ability to communicate with, understand, and motivate individuals and groups
- Conceptual skills: Skills that have to do with thinking in the abstract
- Diagnostic skills: Skills that involve understanding cause-and-effect relationships and recognizing the optimal solutions to a problem

DECISION-MAKING MODELS

Numerous models have been established to illustrate the decision-making process, including the optimizing decision-making model, the so-called "satisficing" model, the implicit favorite model, organizational procedures view, intuitive model, political view, and individual differences perspective.

The first decision-making model, the optimizing model, can be traced back to the "rational manager" view. This is the classic conception of decision making in organizations, developed from the microeconomic notion of a rational, completely informed, single decision maker. In this model of decision making, the decision maker proceeds through six steps that result in the selection of the optimal solution:

Step 1:   Ascertain the need for a decision.
Step 2:   Identify the decision criteria.
Step 3:   Allocate weights to the criteria.
Step 4:   Develop the alternatives.
Step 5:   Evaluate the alternatives.
Step 6:   Select the best alternative.

Lurking behind these steps is the assumption of rationality—the notion that choices are consistent and value-maximizing. The decision maker displays several characteristics:

Goal orientation: The decision maker has a single, well-defined goal that he or she is trying to maximize.

Options: The decision maker is fully comprehensive in his or her ability to assess criteria and alternatives.

Preferences: Rationality assumes that the criteria and alternatives can be assigned numerical values and ranked in a preferential order.

Constancy: The same criteria and alternatives should be obtained every time; the specific decision criteria are constant; and the weights assigned to them are stable over time.

Outcome: The final choice will maximize the outcome because the decision maker will select the alternative that rates the highest.

The second decision-making model uses the satisficing model and world-renowned economist Herbert Simon's concept of bounded rationality. (Simon coined the term *satisfice.* It is presumed to relate to both *satisfy* and *suffice.*) The general premise of bounded rationality is this, as first explained by Simon: Individuals make decisions by constructing simplified models that extract the essential features from problems without capturing all their complexity. A decision maker selects the first solution that is good enough to solve the issue at hand. In other words, satisficing refers to decision making that seeks an acceptable solution, as opposed to an optimal solution.

A third managerial decision-making model is the implicit favorite model. In this decision-making model, the decision maker selects an alternative early in the decision process and tends to be less objective about all the other choices.

A fourth decision-making model referred to as the organizational procedures view stems from the work of R. M. Cyert and J. G. March's *A Behavioral Theory of the Firm,* published in 1963. In this theory, the desire to identify organizational roles, channels of communication, and relationships drives decision making. The formal and informal structure of an organization, its standard operating procedures, and its channels of communication are the important variables influencing decision making.

The fifth managerial decision-making model is called the intuitive model. In this model, the decision maker makes a decision based on his or her experience. In this case, the decision-making process and rational analysis work together.

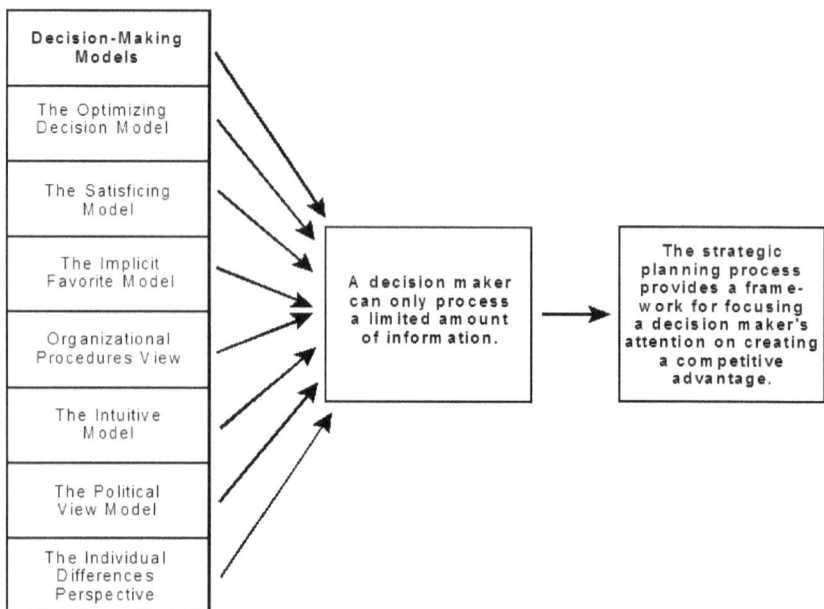

FIGURE 6.3.

According to a sixth model of decision making (the political view), all decisions are determined as an outcome of power and influence. Power, influence, compromise, and negotiation are among various organizational factors and units that influence a decision.

A final model of managerial decision making is the individual differences perspective. In this model, the problem-solving and information-processing capabilities of a decision maker are the most important factors influencing the decision-making process. Important in this theory is the concept of cognitive complexity and the "U-curve." The U-curve hypothesis from H. M. Schroder, M. J. Driver, and S. Steufert (1967) implies that a decision maker can only process a certain amount of information, given a certain environmental complexity (up to a maximum point), after which the information processing of a decision maker is diminished.

The strategic planning process provides a framework for focusing a decision maker's attention on creating a competitive advantage (Figure 6.3).

THE STRATEGIC PLANNING PROCESS

In 1980, Derek F. Abell proposed that the framework of the strategic planning process could be built on the answers to three critical questions:

1. Who is being satisfied?
2. What is being satisfied?
3. How are the needs of the customers being satisfied?

If you determine who is being satisfied, you can identify the customer base (or target market). The other two questions focus attention on the needs of the target market, and how an organization can best meet those needs. In essence, the three questions proposed by Abell form the basis by which organizational decision makers identify or define the purpose of the organization (Figure 6.4).

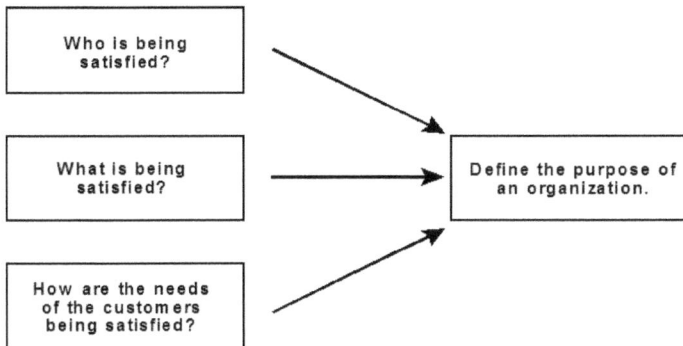

FIGURE 6.4.

Thus, the strategic planning process is utilized to systematically address the questions proposed by Abell; it is also the phase during which managers choose a set of strategies. The strategic planning process consists of five basic steps that can be followed simultaneously.

Step 1.   Formulate the corporate mission and vision statements, and identify the major organizational goals.

Step 2.   Analyze the organization's external competitive environment to identify opportunities and threats.

Step 3.   Analyze the organization's internal operating environment to identify the organization's strengths and weaknesses.

Step 4.   Select strategies that build on the organization's strengths and correct its weaknesses to take advantage of external opportunities and counter external threats.

Step 5.   Implement strategy. Design appropriate organizational structures and control systems to put the organization's chosen strategy into action.

If we look at strategic planning from a different angle, we see that the process can be separated into two dimensions: strategy and operational effectiveness. Michael Porter (1985), a business professor at Harvard University (and probably the leading authority on strategic planning), believes that strategy is a plan for

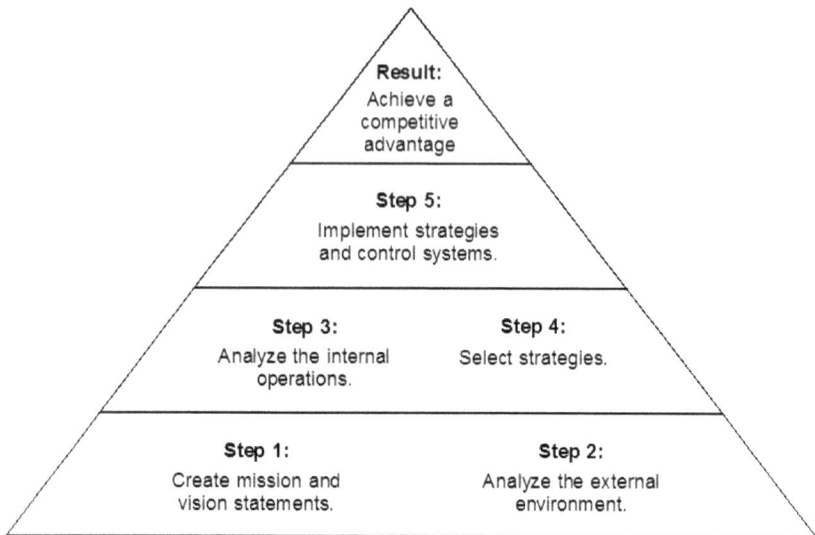

Result:
Achieve a competitive advantage

Step 5:
Implement strategies and control systems.

Step 3:
Analyze the internal operations.

Step 4:
Select strategies.

Step 1:
Create mission and vision statements.

Step 2:
Analyze the external environment.

FIGURE 6.5.

competing in the marketplace, whereas operational effectiveness is the ability to perform operational tasks more efficiently than competitors. The end product of the strategic planning process for an organization should be to establish a competitive advantage over its rivals (Figure 6.5).

COMPETITIVE ADVANTAGE

Some experts contend that competitive advantage is really a strategy to give an organization a distinct advantage over its competition. According to Michael Porter in his 1985 work *Competitive Advantage*, an organization must select a competitive strategy in order to successfully perform at an above-average profitability level because no firm can be all things to all people. Porter proposed three competitive strategy options: cost leadership, a differentiation strategy, and a focus strategy.

Cost leadership is a strategy in which an organization attempts to be the lowest-cost producer in its industry. A firm can obtain a low-cost advantage through efficient operations, economies of scale, technological innovation, low-cost labor, or preferential access to raw materials.

A differentiation strategy occurs when an organization attempts to distinguish itself from its industry competitors within a broad market. To achieve a differentiation strategy, an organization strives to obtain a unique position in the marketplace by emphasizing high quality, extraordinary service, an innovative product design, technological capability, or an unusually positive brand image. The key is that the unique position that the company is attempting to establish must be significantly different from its rivals to justify a price premium that exceeds the cost of differentiating.

A focus strategy is when an organization wants to establish an advantage in a narrow market segment. The focus strategy utilizes either a cost advantage or a differentiation approach aimed at a narrow market segment.

In order to achieve long-term success, an organization must sustain its competitive advantage. Tactics that organizations use to achieve a long-run competitive advantage include establishing barriers to entry, such as patents, copyrights, trademarks, or economies of scale. Firms sometimes lower prices to gain market share, tie up suppliers with exclusive contracts, or lobby Congress to impose trade restrictions designed to limit foreign competition.

Underlying Porter's three competitive strategies are the generic building blocks of competitive advantage, as described by Charles W. L. Hill and Gareth R. Jones (1998):

1. Superior efficiency is about converting inputs into outputs. Inputs are the basic factors of production, such as labor, land, capital, management, and technological know-how. Outputs are the goods and services that an organization produces. The more efficiently an organization can convert inputs into outputs, the higher the productivity level of that organization.

The organization with the highest level of productivity in an industry typically has the lowest costs of production, and therefore gains a competitive advantage.

2. The impact of superior product quality on competitive advantage is two-fold. First, providing high-quality products increases the value of those products in the eyes of the consumer (target market) that allows the firm to charge a higher price. The second impact of high quality on competitive advantage comes from the greater efficiency and lower unit cost it brings.

3. Superior innovation is the most important of the building blocks of competitive advantage. Innovation can be defined as anything new or novel about the way a company operates or about the products it produces. Innovative organizations provide consumers with products that are not available from other firms. That lack of availability allows the organization to charge a premium for its product. In addition, innovative organizations can build brand loyalty, which makes it more difficult for rivals to gain market share.

4. Superior customer service or responsiveness is achieved by identifying and satisfying the needs of the consumers (target market) better than any other organization. Superior customer responsiveness includes such activities as quality, customization, response time, design, and superior service before and after the sale.

Organizations that focus on the building blocks of competitive advantage increase the probability of improving the firm's bottom line (Figure 6.6). When everything else is all said and done, increasing the bottom line is the bottom line!

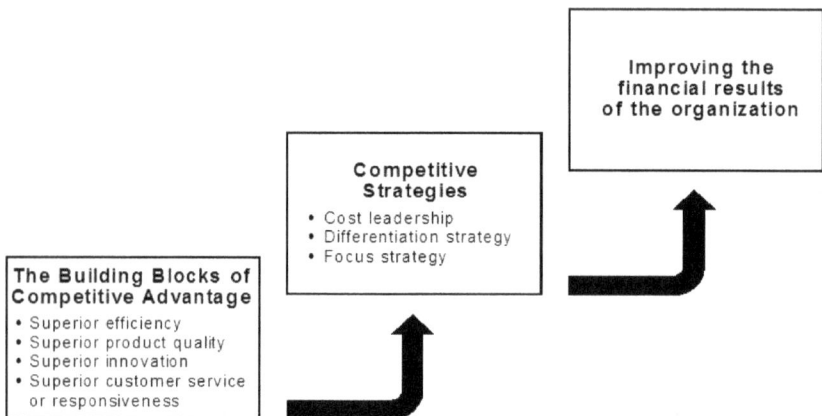

The Building Blocks of Competitive Advantage
- Superior efficiency
- Superior product quality
- Superior innovation
- Superior customer service or responsiveness

Competitive Strategies
- Cost leadership
- Differentiation strategy
- Focus strategy

Improving the financial results of the organization

FIGURE 6.6.

OUTPUT VALUE CREATION AND COMPETITIVE ADVANTAGE

Another important concept connected with the building blocks of competitive advantage is the notion of output value creation—the value of the product or service produced by an organization. An organization creates output value by developing a strategic plan that focuses on the building blocks of competitive advantage. This plan should address the needs of the target market and the employees. In this context, the target market will be specifically referred to as a group of people for which an organization designs, implements, and maintains a strategic plan intended to meet the needs of that group, resulting in mutually satisfying exchanges. The output value generated by an organization is measured by the equation $V = B/P$ (the letter V represents value; B represents perceived and/or actual benefits; and P represents the price of the product). A higher output value as perceived by the target market increases the probability of gaining market share and improving profitability.

OUTPUT VALUE CREATION, THE IMPORTANCE OF THE EMPLOYEES, AND CREATING A GREAT WORKPLACE

Lurking beneath the equation $V = B/P$ is the ability of the workforce and individual employees to create product benefits in an efficient manner. Thus, the lesson to be learned is that employee performance drives the value creation process, and the key to unlocking employee performance is establishing an organization that is a great workplace (Figure 6.7).

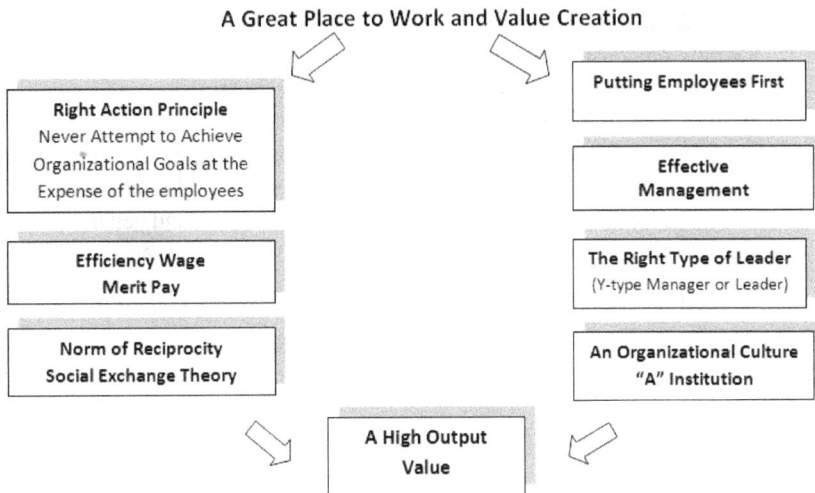

A Great Place to Work and Value Creation

Right Action Principle	Putting Employees First
Never Attempt to Achieve Organizational Goals at the Expense of the employees	
	Effective Management
Efficiency Wage Merit Pay	The Right Type of Leader (Y-type Manager or Leader)
Norm of Reciprocity Social Exchange Theory	An Organizational Culture "A" Institution

A High Output Value

FIGURE 6.7.

Given the critical link between the elements of a great workplace and the value creation process, how do we describe a great workplace? First, a great workplace is not Camelot, for Camelot is a mystical place that only exists in mankind's collective imagination. In Camelot, all wrongs are righted, all injustices are corrected, and evil in any form is eventually overcome by the power of goodness.

So if not Camelot, what is a great workplace? Simply put, an organization that is a great workplace has the following features.

- Adequate and fair compensation for all employees (managerial and non-managerial) based upon merit performance at the individual, group, and organizational level. This includes protection against being laid off or terminated.
- A safe, healthy, comfortable and attractive workplace that is equipped with adequate resources to perform the required job tasks
- Challenging and mutually agreed-upon goals at the individual, group, and organizational level. This includes clearly stated rules and expectations as well as a clear chain of command.
- Jobs that develop human capacities and provide a chance for personal growth and financial security
- A social environment that accepts and promotes each employee's personal identity and characteristics (within reasonable behavior and ethical limits)
- A workplace free from prejudice and based upon merit
- An organizational culture based upon a sense of community, upward mobility, and constitutionalism (the rights of personal privacy, dissent, and due process)
- A work role that minimizes infringement on personal leisure time and family needs outside of normal work hours
- Socially responsible organizational actions
- Job autonomy, meaning working without close supervision and being free to make decisions about one's job independently
- Control over the work process, including the pace, schedule, and demands of the job, and acquisition of new knowledge, skills, and/or abilities
- Opportunities to work and interact with other personnel and departments as well as being able to help others improve their job performance

Organizational decision makers who decide to move beyond a normal company approach and build a great workplace will be among the few willing to travel down that road, but for those willing to do so, the personal and organizational rewards are limitless.

SUMMING IT UP

At its basic level, high performance essentially revolves around knowing how the abilities of each employee differ and using that knowledge to increase the likelihood that any employee will consistently perform his or her job well. Employee job performance begins the "chain" of workplace activity that determines the level of productivity that a group or organization will eventually achieve. Productive environments at the group or organizational level are linked to and depend on the performance of each employee. Like any link in a chain, the productivity that a group or organization can achieve will only be as high as the weakest link in the chain of workplace activity. Group accomplishments and organizational productivity are a function of individual accomplishments and productivity.

Generally, how well an employee performs on the job will be reflective of the employee's intellectual and physical abilities, as well as the job fit between an employee's abilities and the job task. Intellectual ability refers to an employee's capability to do mental activities. The seven most frequently cited dimensions making up intellectual abilities are listed below:

1. Number aptitude is the ability to do speedy and accurate arithmetic.
2. Verbal comprehension is the ability to understand what is read or heard and the relationship between the words.
3. Perceptual speed is the ability to identify visual similarities and differences quickly and accurately.
4. Inductive reasoning is the ability to identify a logical sequence in a problem and then to solve the problem.
5. Deductive reasoning is the ability to use logic and assess the implications of an argument.
6. Spatial visualization is the ability to imagine how an object would look if its position in space were changed.
7. Memory is the ability to retain and recall past experiences.

Physical ability refers to the stamina, dexterity, strength, and similar characteristics that are required to perform a task. The nine basic abilities involved in the performance of physical tasks are listed below, from the same source:

1. Dynamic strength is the ability to exert muscular force repeatedly or continuously over time.
2. Trunk strength is the ability to exert muscular strength using the trunk (particularly abdominal) muscles.
3. Static strength is the ability to exert force against external objects.

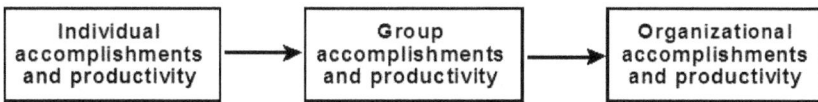

Individual accomplishments and productivity	→	Group accomplishments and productivity	→	Organizational accomplishments and productivity

(A group refers to a department or major function within an organization.)

FIGURE 6.8. Chain of Workplace Activity that Influences Productivity

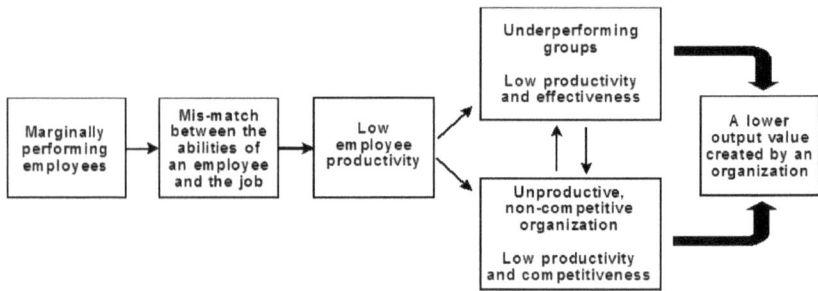

(A group refers to a department or major function within an organization.)

FIGURE 6.9.   The employee ability–job match is out of equilibrium when…

4.   Explosive strength is the ability to expend a maximum of energy in one or a series of explosive acts.
5.   Extent flexibility is the ability to move the trunk and back muscles as far as possible.
6.   Dynamic flexibility is the ability to make rapid, repeated flexing movements.
7.   Body coordination is the ability to coordinate the simultaneous actions of different parts of the body.
8.   Balance is the ability to maintain equilibrium, despite forces pulling one off-balance.
9.   Stamina is the ability to continue maximum effort when prolonged effort is required over time.

To maximize employee performance, you must match the intellectual and physical abilities of an employee to the job. When the employee ability–job match is out of equilibrium because the employee's abilities exceed or are not sufficient to perform the task, the performance level of the employee will be marginal, at best (Figure 6.9). Marginally performing employees result in underperforming groups and an unproductive, noncompetitive organization.

On the other hand, when the employee ability–job match is in equilibrium, an unproductive workplace can be transformed into a productive environment that generates a high output value. This transformation requires a commitment to building a great workplace. Within this type of work environment, employee productivity is nourished and strengthened. As employee productivity gains strength and expands, output value increases, just like the trunk and branches of a tree stretch further and further towards the sky when its roots are firmly planted in fertile ground (see Figure 6.10).

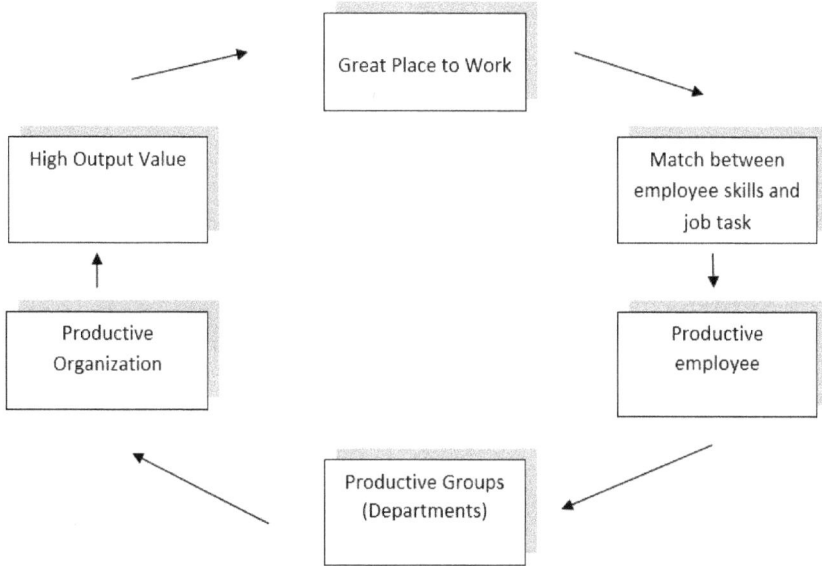

Figure 6.10. Individual, Group (Department), Organizational Success and a Great workplace

Given the importance of a great workplace, how do we know when one exists? Here is how Thompson and Stickland (2003) put it:

> Organizations with a spirit of high performance typically are intensely people-oriented, and they reinforce their concern for individual employees on every conceivable occasion in every conceivable way. They treat employees with dignity and respect, train each employee thoroughly, encourage employees to use their own initiative and creativity in performing their work, set reasonable and clear performance standards, hold managers at every level responsible for developing the people who report to them, and grant employees enough autonomy to stand out, excel, and contribute. Creating a results-oriented organizational culture generally entails making champions out of the people who turn in winning performances.

The bottom line is that a great workplace supports such a high quality of work life that those individuals who work there never want to leave, for they can find no better place to work.

CHAPTER 7

DOES YOUR ORGANIZATION MEASURE UP?

In the previous chapter, we learned that establishing a great workplace creates an environment where productivity can thrive and the output value-creation process can flourish, just like a long-overdue rain can transform a barren patch of land into a garden oasis. Gaining an understanding of the value-creation process was a vital step forward in our understanding of the importance of a great workplace. However, our final destination involves moving beyond the value-creation process, for ultimately we must uncover a measurement tool that can quantify whether an organization is a great workplace or something else.

So, like a group of explorers, we must continue to push ahead in our quest to unlock the characteristics of a great workplace. However, sometimes to move forward one needs to look back at what has already been uncovered. It is peculiar but true that when one is searching for something or unsure of a particular course of action, the best approach for determining what to do is often to examine what has already taken place in the past. Then the path to the future becomes clear. So here's what we know so far about a great workplace.

- Everything regarding a great workplace begins with the right action principle.

Is Your Organization a Great Workplace? pages 49–53.
49

- In a great workplace, a norm of reciprocity exists between the organization and its employees (managerial and non-managerial). As a consequence, the principles embedded within social exchange theory are quite evident within a great workplace.
- Efficiency wages are paid, and adequate and fair benefits are provided with the goal of achieving financial security for all employees (managerial and non-managerial).
- The workplace is free from prejudice, and a truly functioning merit pay system is in place at the individual, group, and organizational level.
- An organizational culture "A" exists.
- A "putting employees first" philosophy is incorporated in organizational policies, practices, and procedures.
- The right type of leaders (Y-type leaders) are in positions of authority throughout the organization; there is no place for CREEPS.
- Effective management principles are followed.
- A safe, healthy, comfortable, well-equipped, and attractive workplace exists.
- Challenging and mutually agreed-upon goals at the individual, group, and organizational level are established. This includes clearly stated rules and expectations as well as a clear chain of command.
- Jobs are designed to develop human capacities, meaning that knowledge, skills, and abilities are being enhanced in order to provide a chance for personal growth and greater financial opportunities.
- A social environment is established that accepts and promotes each employee's personal identity and characteristics (within reasonable behavior and ethical limits).
- The organizational culture is based upon a sense of community, upward mobility, and constitutionalism (the rights of personal privacy, dissent, and due process).
- Job tasks minimize infringement on personal leisure time and family needs outside of normal work hours.
- The organization engages in socially responsible actions.
- Job autonomy is encouraged within reasonable limits (meaning working without close supervision and being free to make decisions about one's job independently).
- Employee control over the work process (including the pace, setting one's own schedule, the demands of the job, and acquiring new knowledge, skills, and abilities) is fostered within reasonable limits.
- Opportunities to work and interact with other personnel and departments as well as being able to help others improve their job performance are part of the organizational culture.

TABLE 7.1. Is Your Organization a Great workplace Measurement Form

Variables	Points for Variable	Does the Organization have the variable (Yes or No)	Organization Points
Is your organization governed by the right action principle?	2 for yes 0 for no		
Efficiency wages are paid and adequate and fair benefits are provided with the goal of achieving financial security for all employees (managerial and non-managerial).	1 for yes 0 for no		
The workplace is free from prejudice, and a truly functioning merit pay system is in place at the individual, group, and organizational level.	1 for yes 0 for no		
An organizational culture "A" exists.	1 for yes 0 for no		
A "putting employees first" philosophy is incorporated in organizational policies, practices, and procedures.	1 for yes 0 for no		
The right type of leaders (Y-type leaders) are in positions of authority throughout the organization—there is no place for CREEPS	1 for yes 0 for no		
Effective management principles are followed.	1 for yes 0 for no		
A safe, healthy, comfortable, well-equipped, and attractive workplace exists.	1 for yes 0 for no		
Challenging and mutually agreed-upon goals at the individual, group, and organizational level are established. This includes clearly stated rules and expectations as well as a clear chain of command.	1 for yes 0 for no		
Jobs are designed to develop human capacities, meaning that knowledge, skills, and abilities are being enhanced in order to provide a chance for personal growth and greater financial opportunities.	1 for yes 0 for no		
A social environment is established that accepts and promotes each employee's personal identity and characteristics (within reasonable behavior and ethical limits).	1 for yes 0 for no		
The organizational culture is based upon a sense of community, upward mobility, and constitutionalism (the rights of personal privacy, dissent, and due process).	1 for yes 0 for no		

(continues)

TABLE 7.1. Continued

Variables	Points for Variable	Does the Organization have the variable (Yes or No)	Organization Points
Job tasks minimize infringement on personal leisure time and family needs outside of normal work hours.	1 for yes 0 for no		
The organization engages in socially responsible actions.	1 for yes 0 for no		
Job autonomy is encouraged within reasonable limits (meaning working without close supervision and being free to make decisions about one's job independently).	1 for yes 0 for no		
Employee control over the work process (including the pace, setting one's own schedule, the demands of the job, and acquiring new knowledge, skills, and abilities) is fostered within reasonable limits.	1 for yes 0 for no		
Opportunities to work and interact with other personnel and departments as well as being able to help others improve their job performance are part of the organizational culture.	1 for yes 0 for no		

Given the above characteristics, we can now qualify whether an organization is a great workplace (Table 7.1).

An organization is a great workplace if it scores 16–18 points. An organization can be classified as a Normal Company Approach Plus (+) if its score is 14–15 points. If the organization's score is 12–13 points, then that workplace can be labeled as a Normal Company Approach Minus (–). A Below Normal Company Approach would be a score of 10–11 points. An organization that scores 9 points or below can be identified as a "Let's Get Out of Here as Soon as Possible" company.

SUMMING IT UP

Achieving our final destiny of discovering a measurement tool that captures the essence of a great workplace began by unlocking the elements of a great workplace. Our adventure moved forward by revealing a set of characteristics or variables that described a great workplace and ended by determining how an organization measures up to those variables.

A Great Place to Work (18 to 16 points)

A Normal Company Approach Plus (+) (15 to 14 points)

A Normal Company Approach Minus (-) (13 to 12 points)

Below Normal Company Approach (11 to 10 points)

Let's Get Out of Here as Soon as Possible Company (9 or less points)

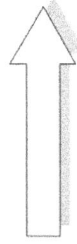

Another methodology for portraying whether an organization is a great workplace and the importance of a productive workplace is summarized in Figure 7.1.

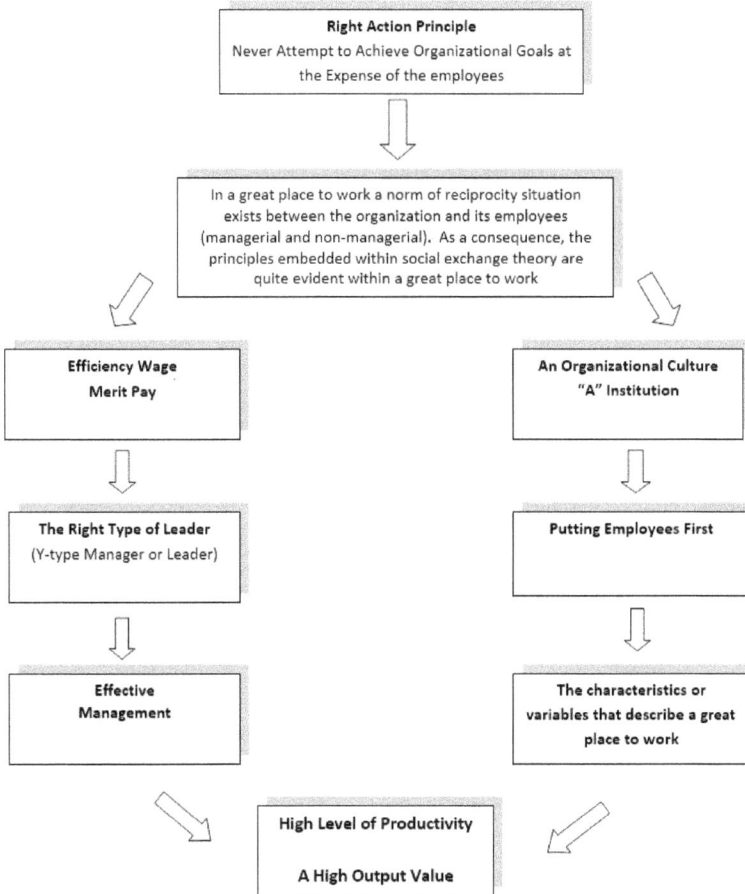

Right Action Principle
Never Attempt to Achieve Organizational Goals at the Expense of the employees

In a great place to work a norm of reciprocity situation exists between the organization and its employees (managerial and non-managerial). As a consequence, the principles embedded within social exchange theory are quite evident within a great place to work

Efficiency Wage Merit Pay

An Organizational Culture "A" Institution

The Right Type of Leader (Y-type Manager or Leader)

Putting Employees First

Effective Management

The characteristics or variables that describe a great place to work

High Level of Productivity

A High Output Value

FIGURE 7.1.   A Great Workplace, Productivity, and Value Creation

CHAPTER 8

DECISION TIME

Let's review a few statements from the book.

Preface

- Greatness requires great achievements, and the issue becomes how can greatness be best achieved: the Normal Company approach or the great workplace approach?

Introduction

- Have you ever worked for an organization where it felt like no one cared about you and that your contribution to the organization was always minimized—or worse, unappreciated?

Chapter 1

- The critical question is: What type of organizational culture or work environment will best support organizational sustainability?
- The issue is: How does an organization craft a great workplace?

Is Your Organization a Great Workplace? pages 55–61.
Copyright © 2015 by Information Age Publishing
55

Chapter 2

- Three critical workplace parameters are (1) managerial attitudes and practices in the workplace, (2) the organizational environment, and (3) the tasks being performed within an organization. The workplace parameters form the foundation of the Organizational Culture Financial Status Model (OCFSM).
- The OCFSM establishes a framework to evaluate the culture of an organization and provides a methodology for improving the financial performance of an organization.
- At the core of the three workplace parameters and the OCFSM is the quality of the employees (managerial and non-managerial) of an organization. Failing to recognize this fact puts the organization in serious jeopardy.

Chapter 3

- Which type of boss would you prefer? The right type of leader (Y-type manager or leader) or a CREEP (X-type of manager or leader)?
- The right type of leader can only emerge from an altruistic approach to life.
- The right type of leader focuses upon the needs of the employees, thereby creating a workplace characterized by highly motivated and productive employees who are focused upon satisfying the needs of the customer. In other words, the right type of leader pursues organizational goals and objectives in such a way that the growth and integrity of people are respected. Other characteristics of the right type of leader include: comfortable with people; puts employees first; open-door cheerleader; no reserved parking place, private washroom, or dining room; common touch; good listener; fair; humble; tough, confronts nasty problems; tolerant of disagreement (respectful of the opinion of others); has strong convictions (altruistic approach to life); trusts people; gives credit, takes blame; prefers personal communication over written communication such as memos, email, or long reports; keeps promises; and thinks there are at least two other people in the organization who would be good CEOs.
- CREEPS (X-type managers or leaders) must always be eliminated from any management or leadership position.

Chapter 4

- My premise is not to blame management for every organizational failure but to suggest that the time has arrived for a paradigm shift in the relationship between management and the employees. Management must come to the realization that organizational performance is enhanced when they view employees as partners, not subordinates; in other words, management must put the employees first—and mean it. The managerial philosophy of putting the employees first and reinforcing that philosophy through the policies and practices established by management is one of the features that distinguish a great workplace from the rest. Management retains the final decision-making authority, but the focus should be upon how an organizational decision impacts the employees for that in turn will influence how the employees feel about the organization, perform their job, and ultimately how they interact with the customer.

- After studying management, leadership, organizational behavior, marketing, and economics since the 1980s and working in numerous administrative positions, I have come to the conclusion that organizations that establish policies and practices that clearly demonstrate a true concern for the employees have set the stage where the employees will be more likely to put forth the maximum effort to take care of the customer, not the minimum.
- Efficient managers are guided by the following principles: (1) craft an organizational vision and mission that is shared and supported by all stakeholders; (2) build the culture of the organization around the right action principle and putting employees first; (3) create a safe, efficient, and effective workplace; (4) develop a collaborative relationship with local, state, national, and international stakeholders; (5) promote ethical conduct; and (6) foster an awareness of the larger cultural, legal, economic, political, and social forces that impact the organization.

Chapter 5

- A high level of job satisfaction, job involvement, and organizational commitment stems from creating a great workplace and matching the physical and intellectual abilities of an employee with the job.
- When employees are well suited for the job, remarkable levels of productivity can be achieved. Productive employees are motivated employees. Motivation refers to an individual's willingness to exert high levels of effort. Employees are willing and able to exert a high level of effort when the employee ability–job match is in equilibrium, when recognition is provided for accomplishments, and when opportunities for advancement are available for those employees who desire that. A motivated workforce sets the stage for organizational success and sustainability. In today's extremely competitive and global business environment, no organization can expect to achieve sustainability without a highly motivated workforce.
- Motivation is about establishing an environment where individuals have the opportunity to grow better every day.

Chapter 6

- The role of strategic planning is to keep an organization on track and focused on the activities that it does best so that it does not drift into mediocrity.
- To accomplish its role, the strategic planning process should always be the same: (1) discover the critical factors in a situation and (2) design a way of coordinating and focusing actions to deal with those factors.
- Systems engineering pioneer Andrew Sage defines managerial decision making as the processes of thought and action involving an irrevocable allocation of resources that culminates in choice behavior. The quality of a decision depends on how well the decision maker is able to acquire and evaluate information.
- Organizations that focus on the building blocks of competitive advantage increase the probability of improving the firm's bottom line.
- Another important concept connected with the building blocks of competitive advantage is the notion of output value creation—the value of the product or service produced by an organization.
- Lurking beneath the equation $V = B/P$ is the ability of the workforce and individual employees to create product benefits in an efficient manner. Thus, the lesson to be learned is that employee performance drives the value-creation process, and the key to unlocking employee performance is establishing an organization that is a great workplace.
- At its basic level, high performance essentially revolves around knowing how the abilities of each employee differ and using that knowledge to increase the likelihood that any employee will consistently perform his or her job well. Employee job performance begins the chain of workplace activity that determines the level of productivity that a group or organization will eventually achieve. Productive environments at the group or organizational level are linked to and depend on the performance of each employee. Like any link in a chain, the productivity that a group or organization can achieve can only be as high as the weakest link in the chain of workplace activity. Group accomplishments and organizational productivity are a function of individual accomplishments and productivity.
- To maximize individual accomplishments and productivity, you must match the intellectual and physical abilities of an employee to the job.

Chapter 7

- Here's what we know about a great workplace.
  - Everything regarding a great workplace begins with the right action principle.

- In a great workplace, a norm of reciprocity situation exists between the organization and its employees (managerial and non-managerial). As a consequence, the principles embedded within social exchange theory are quite evident within a great workplace.
- Efficiency wages are paid, and adequate and fair benefits are provided with the goal of achieving financial security for all employees (managerial and non-managerial).
- The workplace is free from prejudice, and a truly functioning merit pay system is in place at the individual, group, and organizational level.
- An organizational culture "A" exists.
- A "putting employees first" philosophy is incorporated in organizational policies, practices, and procedures.
- The right type of leaders (Y-type leaders) are in positions of authority throughout the organization; there is no place for CREEPS.
- Effective management principles are followed.
- A safe, healthy, comfortable, well-equipped, and attractive workplace exists.
- Challenging and mutually agreed-upon goals at the individual, group, and organizational level are established. This includes clearly stated rules and expectations as well as a clear chain of command.
- Jobs are designed to develop human capacities meaning that knowledge, skills, and abilities are being enhanced in order to provide a chance for personal growth and greater financial opportunities.
- A social environment is established that accepts and promotes each employee's personal identity and characteristics (within reasonable behavior and ethical limits).
- The organizational culture is based upon a sense of community, upward mobility, and constitutionalism (the rights of personal privacy, dissent, and due process).
- Job tasks minimize infringement on personal leisure time and family needs outside of normal work hours.
- The organization engages in socially responsible actions.
- Job autonomy is encouraged within reasonable limits (meaning working without close supervision and being free to make decisions about one's job independently).
- Employee control over the work process (including the pace, setting one's own schedule, the demands of the job, and acquiring new knowledge, skills, and abilities) is fostered within reasonable limits.
- Opportunities to work and interact with other personnel and departments as well as being able to help others improve their job performance are part of the organizational culture.
- According to the "Is Your Organization a Great workplace Measurement Form," an organization is a great workplace if it scores 16–18 points. An

organization can be classified as a Normal Company Approach Plus (+) if its score is 14–15 points. If the organization's score is 12–13 points, then that workplace can be labeled as a Normal Company Approach Minus (–). A "Below Normal Company Approach" would be a score of 10–11 points. An organization that scores 9 points or fewer can be identified as a "Let's Get Out of Here as Soon as Possible" company.

Given these statements, shouldn't we all be wondering why organizational decision makers tend to resist implementing much of the information contained in this book? Wouldn't an organization that is a great workplace be more productive and competitive in the marketplace? The answer is obvious; thus, the question becomes, why aren't more organizations a great workplace? For organizational decision makers it is decision time: a normal company approach or a great workplace approach?

SUMMING IT UP

I hope you don't mind if a nonfiction author tries his hand at creating a brief tale about life and self-discovery.

A Tale About Life and Self-Discovery

As I looked into the night sky, I wanted to reach up and touch the stars. But as I raised my hands towards the heavens, I knew that the sparkling objects seemingly adrift in the calm, dark waters of a faraway ocean were many light years away.

How far does the universe extend? What are its boundaries? Does the universe have any boundaries? As these questions fueled my imagination, I suddenly felt as if mankind was being drawn back to the days of Columbus, who, standing upon the shores of the mighty Atlantic, dreamed of discovering a New World. A world that would forever establish the boundaries of the Earth—like a painting set within its frame.

With my thoughts still drifting among the stars, I wondered what new adventures await our species: What new mysteries would mankind uncover? But most of all I was trying to visualize how our lives would change as we continue to unlock what was once unknown.

The unknown, the gray area of life, offers so many mysteries, the most haunting of which is the quest to uncover the meaning of life. Does life have a purpose? Is there a natural order to the universe? Is there a universal plan? Can the answers to these questions be found in some faraway location in the universe? Do the stars that dot the heavenly landscape mark the trail to that location, like glimmering points on a celestial map, or will mankind be destined to roam upon many paths that never quite lead us to the answers we so desperately seek?

As these thoughts completely engulfed my consciousness, like a thick fog rolling across a field swallowing up everything in sight, the glowing light of the sun began to slowly appear near the horizon, and soon the darkness gave way to the birth of a new day. As the soothing rays of the rising sun gently reached out and touched my face, I suddenly realized that the meaning of life is not found by searching through some remote corner of the universe but will only be revealed through an exploration of the soul. Life is about what we think, what we believe in, how we live our daily lives, and most important, how we treat others.

Life is a voyage of self-discovery, and the heavenly light of the stars seems to possess an almost mystical ability to inspire each of us to search deep within our souls and probe for the answers that explain why we are the way we are. This is an intensive, private inquiry that will eventually unmask our "real" identity as every layer of our "outer being" gets peeled away until our "inner being" lies totally exposed. Only after such a journey will our minds and hearts be opened to the realization of how we either positively or negatively influence the environment around us.

At the heart of our quest to uncover what constitutes a great workplace is the notion of how we interact with others, for it is the quality of that interaction that distinguishes a great workplace from other workplaces. The bottom line is that it is our behaviors, attitudes, and actions that ultimately determine whether a great workplace can exist.

In *Just After Sunset,* Stephen King wrote, "No, he had to decide where the road was, and where it was going" (2008, p. 180). Organizational decision makers must decide if they want to establish a great workplace. The personal, economic, and organizational benefits will reward those decision makers willing to follow the path we travelled in this book.

It's decision time!

CHAPTER 9

FINAL COMMENT

In the end, it is not about you (the leader or manager); it is about the people who work for you. This workplace philosophy is embedded within the right action principle.

If your organization is guided by the right action principle, your organization is probably a great workplace, productive, generating a high output value, and outperforming your competition in the marketplace.

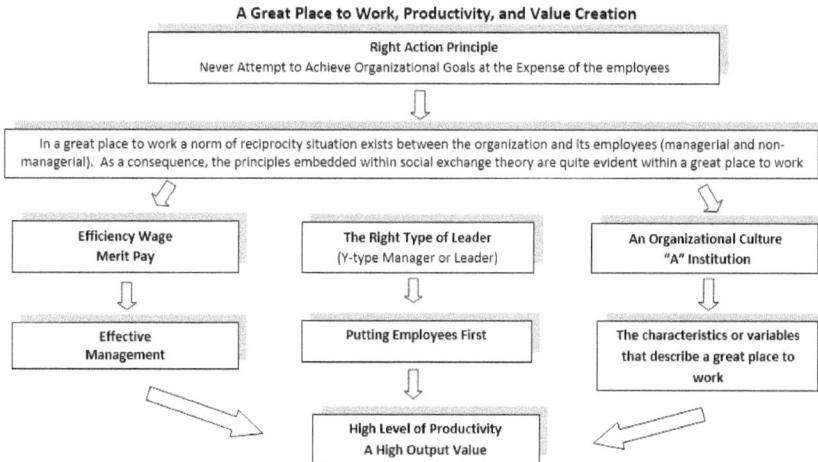

A Great Place to Work, Productivity, and Value Creation

Right Action Principle
Never Attempt to Achieve Organizational Goals at the Expense of the employees

⇩

In a great place to work a norm of reciprocity situation exists between the organization and its employees (managerial and non-managerial). As a consequence, the principles embedded within social exchange theory are quite evident within a great place to work

Efficiency Wage **Merit Pay**	**The Right Type of Leader** (Y-type Manager or Leader)	**An Organizational Culture** **"A" Institution**
⇩	⇩	⇩
Effective **Management**	**Putting Employees First**	**The characteristics or variables that describe a great place to work**

High Level of Productivity **A High Output Value**

Is Your Organization a Great Workplace? page 63.

REFERENCES

Baumol, W. J., & Blinder, A. S. (2000). *Economics: Principles and policy*. Orlando, FL: Harcourt College Publishers.

Byham, W. C., & Cox, J. (1988). *Zapp! The lightning of empowerment*. New York, NY: Fawcett Columbine Book.

Crosby, P. B. (1986). *Running things: The art of making things happen*. New York, NY: Mentor.

Cyert, R. M. & March, J. G. (1963). *A behavioral theory of the firm*. New York, NY: Wiley/Blackwell.

Fullan, M. (2003). *The moral imperative of school leadership*. Thousand Oaks, CA: Corwin Press.

Fullan, M. (2005). *Leadership & sustainability: System thinkers in action*. Thousand Oaks, CA: Corwin Press/Sage.

Fullan, M. (2007). *The new meaning of educational change* (4th Ed.). NY: Teachers College Press.

Galbraith, J. K. (1983). *The anatomy of power*. Boston, MA: Houghton Mifflin Company.

Galbraith, J. K., & Goodman, J. (Eds.). (1998). *Letters to Kennedy*. Cambridge, MA: Harvard University Press.

Gitman, L. J., & McDaniel, C. (2003). *The best of the future of business*. Mason, OH: Thomson/South-Western.

Gouldner, A. W. (1960). The norm of reciprocity: A preliminary statement. *American Sociological Review, 25*, 161–177.

Is Your Organization a Great Workplace? pages 65–66.

Hellriegel D., Slocum, J., & Woodman, R. (1995). *Organizational behavior* (7th ed.). St. Paul, MN: West publishing Company.

Hill, C., & Jones, G. R. (1998). *Strategic management: An integrated approach.* Boston, MA: Houghton Mifflin.

Johnston, B. (1994). Educational administration in the postmodern age. In S. Maxcy (Ed.), *Postmodern school leadership: Meeting the crisis in educational administration* (pp. 115–131). Westport, CT: Praeger

Kent, S. (2005, September 6). Happy workers are the best workers. *Wall Street Journal,* p. A20.

King, S. (2008). *Just after sunset.* New York, NY: Pocket Books.

Koontz, D. (2008). *Your heart belongs to me.* NY: Bantam.

Koontz, H. (1961). The management theory jungle. In M. Matteson & J. Ivancevich (Eds.), *Management & organizational behavior classics* (7th ed., pp.). Boston, MA: Irwin/McGraw-Hill.

Laws, S. (1987). *The wyrm.* New York, NY: Leisure Books.

Levy, M. (2004). *Where else would you rather be?* Champaign, IL: Sports Publishing.

Manzo, K. (2006, October 25). Voyager sails into market for reading. *Education Week,* pp. 1, 20.

Mintzberg, H. (1973). *The nature of managerial work.* New York, NY: Harper and Row.

Moorhead, G., & Griffin, R. W. (1995). *Organizational behavior: Managing people and organizations* (4th ed.). Boston, MA: Houghton Mifflin.

Morgan, G. (1997). *Images of organization.* Thousand Oaks, CA: Sage.

Ouchi, W. G., (1981). *Theory Z: How American business can meet the Japanese challenge.* Reading, MA: Addison-Wesley.

Peters, T., & Austin, N. (1985). *A passion for excellence.* New York, NY: Random House.

Porter, M. (1985). *Competitive advantage: Creating and sustaining superior performance.* New York, NY: The Free Press.

Robbins, S. (2001). *Organizational behavior* (9th ed.). Upper Saddle River, NJ: Prentice-Hall.

Schein, E. (1983). The role of the founder in creating organizational culture. *Organizational Dynamics,* 14.

Seyfarth, J. T. (2005). *Human resources management for effective schools* (4th ed.). Boston, MA: Pearson/Allyn and Bacon.

Thompson, A., & Stickland, III, A. J. (2003). *Strategic management: Concepts and cases.* New York, NY: McGraw-Hill Irwin.

Toffler, A. (1971). *Future shock.* NY: Bantam Books.

Twomey, D., Jennings, M., & Fox, I. (2005). *Anderson's Business Law and the Legal Environment* (Standard Volume, 19th Ed.). Mason, OH: Thompson-South-Western.

Umback, P. D. (2007). How effective are they? Exploring the impact of contingent faculty on undergraduate education. *The Review of Higher Education, 30*(2), 91–123.

Weber, L. (2013, June 11). What makes staff stay longer? Here's one company's answer. *Wall Street Journal,* p. B3.

www.ingramcontent.com/pod-product-compliance
Lightning Source LLC
Chambersburg PA
CBHW070410200326
41518CB00011B/2143